MW01594812

The Elizabeth Powell Site (41FB269)

Fort Bend County, Texas

Houston Archeological Society
Report No. 25, Part 3
September, 2014

Part 3 Authors:
Elizabeth K. Aucoin
Richard L. Gregg
Thomas L. Nuckols
Robert T. Shelby

Editors:
Elizabeth K. Aucoin
Linda L. Swift

Houston Archeological Society

www.txhas.org

Cover Illustration: Examples of ceramics recovered at 41FB269. Photos by Richard L. Gregg.

Houston Archeological Society, Report No. 25, Part 3

This publication is Part 3 in a 3-part report on excavations at the Elizabeth Powell Site (41FB269). Digital copies of the entire report, Parts 1, 2, and 3, can be purchased by visiting the Houston Archeological Society web site at www.txhas.org, where current prices, availability, and ordering instructions will be posted. The Society can also be reached at PO Box 130631, Houston, TX 77219-0631.

Dedication

This document, HAS Report No. 25, including all its parts, is dedicated to the memory of those members of the Houston Archeological Society who are no longer with us who contributed their time, talent and resources, in varying degrees, to help make the Elizabeth Powell project possible. These individuals include Frank Brezik Jr., Richey Ebersole, Bill McClure, Don McReynolds, Mary K Merriman, Bernard Naman, David Pettus, Dudgeon Walker, and Father Edward Bader, CSB.

Acknowledgements

HAS acknowledges Lise Darst, landowner, who allowed access to the site over a 6-year period, as well as Joe Hudgins, who maintained landowner communication and arranged for access when needed, and last but certainly not least, Sheldon Kindall, who served as field site supervisor. Special thanks to everyone who labored in the field and the lab; this report reflects your dedication to Texas archeology.

Table of Contents

Figures

Maps

Tables

Illustrations

Chapter 1
Ceramics

Text and Photography by Richard L. Gregg

Introduction

Ceramics is a major and important category of artifacts found at the Elizabeth Powell site, 41FB269. Sherds were found in almost all pits. The main interest temporally for this site is the time of occupation by the Powells, from about 1828 to 1836 (Shelby 2007:13-20). Fortunately, this time period, along with the years just before and after, was an era of relatively fast changes in ceramic technology and fashions, and so analysis of the ceramics from the site has the potential to provide significant information concerning the Powell occupation.

Basic sections of this report concern laboratory and analysis procedures, pattern names and dates, and the various types of ceramics found at the site. With the latter, there are sections for each of the main ceramic types, as distinguished by decoration. Categorization by paste type or similar characteristics is avoided because such procedures are generally more confusing to the non-specialist and do not lead to better insight of site usage in this case.

Discussion of ceramics unavoidably involves many ceramics-specific terms, some of which may not be familiar to the reader. Rather than frequently interrupting the discussion to define or explain terms, we have added a Glossary of terms at the end of this chapter.

Laboratory and Analysis Procedures

About 2200 sherds, weighing a total of about 10 kg (22 lb), were recovered. The sherds were washed in water using a soft brush and then air dried. A log number was assigned to all the sherds from a given pit and level. Sherds were labeled with India ink on their (broken) edges with the site number, the log number, and a serial number. The latter was used to differentiate sherds with the same log number, i.e., from the same pit and level. Those too small for labeling were bagged in plastic, and the site, log, and serial numbers were written on the bag. Those sherds which crossmended (fitted together) were joined using PVA (polyvinyl acetate) dissolved in acetone as an adhesive. If three or more crossmended, a unique Cluster Number was assigned and a full-scale outline sketch of the cluster was made showing the joints and giving the log-serial designation of each sherd. In this way, provenience would not be lost when log-numbered edges were covered by crossmending. A total of 48 clusters were obtained. In several cases, a substantial portion of a plate, cup plate, saucer, or pitcher was obtained through crossmending. Also, a few small clusters consisted of a number of crossmended small sherds. The total number of crossmended sherds was 426.

A spreadsheet was generated to help investigate various aspects of the ceramics. For each sherd, characteristics such as provenience, type of decoration, color(s), pattern, and cluster number were recorded where applicable. Presence of rim, footrim, and other identifiable vessel shape attributes were noted. Specific vessel forms were noted where discernible; these were generally plate, platter, cup, mug, saucer, cup plate, pitcher, and bowl. Other hollow ware forms such as sugar bowls and soup tureens were generally not recognized because of the difficulty in distinguishing among the various hollow ware forms from small sherds and because of the scarcity of such forms at this site. Estimates of size of vessels were made where such could be done with reasonable accuracy. In particular, diameters of round vessels such as plates, cup plates, and cups were made when a sufficient portion of the lip was present. The diametral measurements were facilitated by use of a transparency with printed concentric rings of appropriate diameters. This allowed a fairly accurate diameter to be determined from relatively small sherds or clusters by merely matching the sherd edge curvature to that of a ring. In addition, edge diameters, footring diameters, base diameters, and sometimes other diameters were measured. Heights of vessels were also measured when possible. The sorting capabilities of the spreadsheet software facilitated the obtaining of various statistics on the ceramics.

Pattern Names and Dates

In this report, especially in the section on transferware, emphasis is given to pattern names and their date ranges. One must always be mindful of the pitfalls in using these characteristics for interpreting site usage. Until later in the nineteenth century, manufacturers only occasionally gave names to the designs on their wares; and this was usually done via printed or impressed back marks. Thus many of the earlier series and patterns for which back mark names have not been discovered have, over the years, been given names by collectors. Thus it is not uncommon for a pattern or even a series to have more than one name. Likewise, many of the various patterns and series have been attributed to certain manufacturers, but some of these have been shown to be incorrect. Examples of this are several series formerly widely attributed to Clews which now appear to have been made by Davenport (Arman 1999). In this report no distinction is made as to whether a series or pattern name is actual or attributed.

Pattern dates given in ceramics references are often manufacturing dates, and these have been derived for the most part from secondary sources, especially known dates of ownership or operation of a factory. For example, the dates for some Davenport series or patterns are often given the very wide range of 1794-1887 (as are some in this report), whereas for specific sherds the date range may be reduced considerably because of other factors such as color, back stamp, or importer's mark (as for the 1830-1835 range for the Davenport Florentine Fountain series sherd in this report). The actual dates of manufacture for a specific pattern are usually not known. Also, a vessel may have been in use or kept as an heirloom for many years, and even at another location, before it was discarded at the site.

Another caution in interpreting ceramics at a site is the use of sherd counts and weights. Vessels may be broken up into many or only a few sherds, so counts and weights are not necessarily representative of the ceramics use at a site. Furthermore, utilitarian ceramics, notably stoneware and yellow ware vessels, are much larger and heavier than tableware and teaware vessels, and usually have larger, much heavier sherds, so comparison of count and weight data between these two categories must be made with caution.

There are various ways in which ceramics have been characterized and classified. In this report, the classification is by type of decoration, except in a few cases in which other properties may be important in site interpretation. This gives a classification procedure which is closer to the way in which the Powell site inhabitants probably characterized their pottery, and avoids complex hierarchies such as develop when, for example, the nature of the paste is used as a prime classifier.

Red Earthenware

A total of 50 red earthenware sherds were recovered at the site. Vessels represented include at least four bowls, one with footring and three without. One of the latter bowls is 6.3 inches in diameter and 2.3 inches in height (Figure 1.1). The bowls are of types made in Colonial Texas as well as in Mexico (personal communication, Anne Fox, 2009).

At least 12 other sherds appear to have come from at least two smaller bowls of diameters perhaps 4 to 6 inches. Both have an olive-colored glaze or slip and glaze over the interior, while one has it also on the exterior (underside) just near the rim and the other on the entire exterior. A like number of sherds appear to be from similar bowls,

Figure 1.1 Red earthenware bowl

but the glaze or slip and glaze has deteriorated to a whitish or, in a few cases, silvery film.

Five other small sherds are decorated. Decoration consists of brown and yellow slip lines. Although these are similar to the decorations of several early types of Mexican unglazed ware, they are glazed.

Figure 1.2 Huejotzingo Wavy Rim Band Green on White sherd

One small sherd of tin-glazed ware (Majolica) was found. It is of the type called Huejotzingo Wavy Rim Band Green on White, which is a Colonial Mexican ware that dates to ca.1775-1825 (Fox and Ulrich 2008:39,100-101; Cargill et al. 2004:68, Figure 6-5g). See Figure 1.2.

Undecorated Whiteware

A large proportion of the sherds found at this site were undecorated whiteware (752 out of 2155 = 35%). The term "whiteware" here includes any CC (cream-colored) ware and pearlware. The word "undecorated" here means no applied decoration; patterns made by molding are not considered decorated. (In the latter 1800s, copper or gold lustre was sometimes applied to otherwise undecorated vessels, especially to those with molded shapes. Such vessels are also designated here as undecorated.) Of course, some of the apparently undecorated sherds may come from undecorated portions of decorated vessels. This is certainly true for sherds of edge-ware vessels, since much of the (complete) vessel is undecorated. However, other types of tableware, such as transferware and hand-painted ware, usually yield few undecorated sherds. Most

Figure 1.3 Henderson & Gaines importer's mark and Davenport maker's mark

of the undecorated whiteware sherds found at this site are small (except for ironstone -- see below) and singular (unmended). Substantial portions of only four vessels were found -- a small pitcher, a carinated bowl, a plate, and a saucer. For the small pitcher, 41 sherds were mended into three clusters of the same vessel. The carinated bowl is 6.2 inches in diameter and 3.2 inches in height; about 30% of the vessel is represented. The plate is complete (3 sherds), 9.25 inches in diameter, and has a maker's mark of "T. P. C. Co." (Potters Co-Operative Co. East Liverpool, Ohio), which dates to the 1880s (Kowalsky and Kowalsky 1999:A118). The saucer, 6.0 inches in diameter, has maker's mark "Clementson Bros England," which dates to 1867-80 (Godden 1991, #905).

Other manufacturers identified by marks are James Edwards (1842-54), T & R Boote (1842-?), and C. C. Thompson Pottery Co., East Liverpool, Ohio (1889-1910). In addition, there were 10 partial maker's marks that were too fragmentary to identify.

One crossmend pair has a copper lustre motif of Reverse Teaberry (Stoltzfus and Snyder 1997:12, 98) with maker's mark of Clementson Bros (1891-1916) KAD No. B531 (Kowalsky and Kowalsky 1999:148). Another sherd with copper lustre motif that is of uncertain pattern may also have the same maker's mark.

An impressed importer's mark of Henderson and Gaines of New Orleans (1836-66) (Black and Brandimarte 1987) is on an undecorated whiteware sherd (Figure 1.3). This mark reads: "MANU-FACTURED -- / HENDERSON & G --." Nearby on this sherd is the impressed maker's mark of "DAVENPORT" with the characteristic anchor and date mark "44," denoting 1844.

During the early 1800s, some manufacturers used the term ironstone for some of their whitewares. The definition of this term varies; here it will refer to what is sometimes called classical ironstone, namely undecorated white ware that is well made and has substantial body thickness; it was produced in the late 1800s.

About 35 (6%) of the undecorated whiteware sherds are classic ironstone. Because of their thickness and quality of body, the sherds of ironstone are generally relatively large.

Some ironstone vessels had subtle molded or embossed "shapes." Often these are difficult to detect or at least distinguish from one another when there are only a few small sherds. Three shapes have been identified at the Powell site: Laurel Shape," "Lily of the Valley," and "Mocho Shape." These are listed in Table 1.1, along with the potter, dates, references, and other data. Note that the word "Shape" is sometimes part of the shape name. This is intentional.

Edgeware

There are 73 edge-decorated sherds, 68 blue and five green. Of the blue sherds, 63 are of the traditional shell-edge variety, with 26 having a scalloped rim and 29 a straight (non-scalloped) rim, and eight being indeterminate. Two clusters, totaling 12 sherds (including six interior ones), plus four other sherds appear to be from the same or identical deep plates or soup plates. The diameter is 10.0 inches and height 1.1 inches. The rim is scalloped. The rest of the blue sherds appear to come from a variety of plates, except for a hollow ware body sherd[1] and a sherd which is thick enough to be classified as from a platter. There are five blue sherds with non-shell-edge decoration; two have dot-and-plume decoration, two leaf, and one floral.

The five green edge-decorated sherds have scalloped shell edge and appear to have quite similar decoration. However, they were found at disparate parts of the site. Two of the sherds have impressed buds. See Figure 1.4.

Both blue and green shell-edge vessels were manufactured from long before the 1828 starting date of the Powell site. Green shell edge was

Figure 1.4 Edgeware; Left to right, top to bottom: Shell-edge plate or soup plate; green with impressed bud; leaf decoration (2), floral; dot and plume (2); hollow ware body sherd

phased out about 1840, but blue continued on until around 1860 (Miller 1995).

Hand-Painted Ceramics

The hand-painted ceramics at this site, 96 sherds, are almost all of the underglaze type. There are 27 sherds, some relatively large, with thickline floral decoration. All are blue except for one polychrome (blue, green, and brown) sherd. One cluster is part of a bowl and another is a London Shape cup of diameter 3.9 inches and height of 2.4 inches (Figure 1.5). There are two large rim sherds from a shallow bowl or bowls of diameter 6.0 inches. The rest of the hand-painted sherds are small and of the fineline polychrome floral type, with cup, mug, and carinated bowl vessel forms represented. Each of the hand-painted fineline sherds shown in Figure 1.6 has an impressed maker's mark of DAVEN-PORT with an anchor (Lockett and Godden 1989: 73:E5) on the reverse side.

---

[1]For an example of edgeware decoration on a hollow ware vessel, see Furniss et al. 1999:118.

Figure 1.5 Hand-painted London Shape cup, thickline floral decoration

Figure 1.6 Hand-painted ceramics by Davenport, fineline polychrome decoration

Figure 1.7 Spatterware

Spatterware

There are three sherds of spatterware, all with the same reddish purple color. One is part of a handle. See Figure 1.7. Spatterware was manufactured in England from approximately 1780 to the 1830s, with peak production from 1810 to the 1830s (McConnell 1990:10,14). There are no sherds of spongeware, which is considered a successor of spatterware (Kelly et al. 2001:7-11).

Transferware

Transfer-printed ware, or transferware, is made by transferring a pattern engraved on a copper plate, via ink and special tissue paper, to a partially fired item of pottery, and then applying glazing compound and completing the firing. In this manner an intricate pattern on the pottery can be obtained which is also protected by glaze. The pattern was applied in several pieces because of the three-dimensional nature of the pottery vessel surface.

Although transferware was manufactured over the full time of interest at this site (1828-present), it was popular from well before 1828 to about 1850. During this time, the Staffordshire area of England produced almost all of the transferware used in this country. Prior to about 1828, almost all transferware was blue in color, because cobalt compounds were all that had been found to withstand the heat of the final (glost) oven. About 1828,

however, a number of other coloring compounds were discovered, and red, green, purple, brown, and black transferware were soon being produced. Later, some multichrome transferware vessels were produced, but these were uncommon, and no multichrome transferware sherds were found at the Powell site. Before about 1828, vessels with various shades of blue were made, and techniques for producing shading within a pattern were developed, such as stippling. One type of transferware was what is called deep blue. It is characterized by very dark blue color. Deep blue was popular from about 1818 to 1828, whereas lighter blues continued on to about 1850.

For more on the development of transferware, see Samford (1997:2-4) and Lockett and Godden (125-135). Copeland (1999:8-12), Copeland (1999:31-32), Neale (2005:10-13), and Williams (2007:27-29) show photos of various steps in the transfer printing process.

For site 41FB269, 760 sherds, 35% of the total, are classified as transferware. This was the largest count of any category, being a few percent more than undecorated (whiteware) sherds. Of these, 42% are (lighter) blue in color, 22% deep blue, 12% red, 9% purple, 8% green, 5% black, and 3% brown. None are multichrome; a few are clobbered (hand painting over transfer print).

A total of 392 (52%) of the transferware sherds were identified as to series or pattern. Table 1.2 lists the 44 transferware series and patterns identified for 41FB269, including numbered patterns assigned by BAS (Pollan et al. 1996) or Blake and Freeman (1998). Patterns were identified with the aid of published

Figure 1.8 Fountain Scenery by W. Adams & Sons

archeological and collector literature, and the comparative collection of the Brazosport Archaeological Society. Of prime importance are the references given in Table 1.2, especially the catalogs of ceramics from Velasco and Quintana (Pollan et al.1996; Blake and Freeman 1998). It is anticipated that future pattern identification will be greatly aided by use of the TCC Pattern Database (n.d.), now under development.

Figure 1.9 Rabbit Hunting, Hunting series by Davenport

Examples of the transferware patterns found are given in Figures 1.8-1.21. The blue Fountain Scenery plate (Figure 1.8) by W. Adams and sons (Snyder 1997:20), from a trash pit, has hardly any use-wear scratches

on it. Either it was broken soon after purchase or it was otherwise not used. It has a diameter of 10.7 inches. The deep blue pattern Rabbit Hunting (Figure 1.9) (minimum two vessels, diameter 7.0 inches) is from the series called Hunting, probably by Davenport. It was discussed in a previous article (Gregg 2006). The pattern Persian by Heath (minimum two vessels) (Williams 2008:271; Williams and Weber 1998:120) is shown in Figure 1.10. They are 9.0-inch plates. The pattern known as The Villagers by Davenport (Snyder 1997:53) is shown in Figure 1.11. It is a 9.0-inch plate.

Three examples of cup plates are shown in Figures 1.12-1.14. The vessel in Figure 1.12, pattern Europa by John and Richard Riley (Arman and Arman 2000b:18-19), has the maker's mark of "RILEY'S Semi China" on the bottom. The pattern Virginia by J & R Clews is shown in Figure 1.13. Figure 1.14 has the deep blue pattern Game Birds by Stubbs (Arman and Arman 2000b:24). The diameters of these cup plates are 3.6, 4.1, and

4.5 inches, respectively[2]. Not shown is a fragmentary cup plate of diameter 4.0 inches from the series Scott's Illustrations by Davenport.

Figure 1.10 Persian by Heath

Figure 1.11 The Villagers by Davenport

Figure 1.12 Europa (cup plate) by Riley

Figure 1.13 Virginia (cup plate)
by J & R Clews

[2] Williams (1978:11-12) sets the limits of size for a ceramic cup plate to be the same as given by Lee and Rose (1948:4) for glass cup plates, namely a diameter of 2 5/8 inches up to but not including 4 1/4 inches. Plates smaller than this are deemed miniatures or toys. Lee and Rose also say that the center well of the cup plate must be large enough to accommodate the base of the cup. This might be interpreted to mean that the diameter of discussion is that of the center well of the cup plate, and thus the Europa vessel is a toy or miniature because its center well is about 2 inches in diameter. However, examination of Lee and Rose's illustrated glass cup plates indicates that "diameter" pertains to the outside diameter of the cup plate. Furthermore, a maker's mark would not be expected on a toy vessel, but may be on a distributor's miniature sample, as suggested by Sue Gross and Sandra Pollan (private communication 2009) of the Brazosport Archaeological Society. Arman and Arman (2000a:5; 2000b:18,33) indicate that this maker's mark does appear on some cup plates, and they also address the subject of toys and miniatures.

Figure 1.14 Game Birds (cup plate) by Stubbs

The sherd cluster in Figure 1.15 provides a good example of pattern naming problems. The cluster is a portion of a soup plate of diameter 10.3 inches in the series by Enoch Wood called Sporting. This pattern is illustrated by Coysh and Henrywood (1989:188) but misnamed Pointer and Quail. In fact, Pointer and Quail is a different pattern in this series and was illustrated by Laidacker (1951:105-6). Neale (2005:34) calls the pattern Shooting with Gun

Figure 1.15 Setter, Sporting series by Enoch Wood

Dogs, even though there is only one dog. Recent articles by Godden (2009) and Siddall (2009) reveal confusion over this pattern. In the TCC Pattern Database (n.d.), previous naming problems were avoided by calling the pattern Setter.

A blue dish of diameter 5.75 inches and height 1.3 inches in the British Scenery series is shown in Figure 1.16. J & W Ridgway is the attributed maker. In Figure 1.17 is a red carinated bowl of diameter 6.0 inches. The pattern and maker are unknown. In Figure 1.18 is a red transferware dish with diameter 5.75 inches; the pattern is "No. 2" (minimum two vessels). The Willow pattern is the best known of transferware patterns. It has been produced in transferware since the late 1700s, became a standardized pattern in the early 1800s, and is still made today (Coysh and Henrywood 1982:402). A number of Willow sub-patterns have been recognized, but they probably would not be helpful in the investigation for the Powell site. There were 37 sherds of Willow found at this site, including seven from what appears to be a soup plate of diameter 9.8 inches. Examples are shown in Figure 1.19.

Examples of other transferware patterns found at the site are shown in Figure 1.20. All of the sherds are unmended. In the top row, left to right, are Franklin's Morals Series (deep blue), Amaryllis (2 sherds, green), unknown (red), Victoria (blue). In the second row are The Holme, Regent's Park pattern by Enoch Wood & Sons (deep blue), Canova (purple), unknown (purple), unknown (blue). In

the bottom row are Fruit and Flowers by Stubbs (2 thick sherds, platter of size 18.5 inches by 15.3 inches, deep blue), and (perhaps) Palmyra (2 sherds, blue).

Transferware Importers' Marks and Pattern Names on Backstamps

Five transferware sherds with partial importers' marks were found. A printed importer's mark of Hill and Henderson (1822-1834) of New Orleans (Black and Brandimarte 1987; cf. Snyder 1995:45) is on a sherd of the second plate of the pattern Rabbit Hunting, in the Hunting series (Figure 1.9). Hill and Henderson was a predecessor of the Henderson and Gaines partnership mentioned earlier. According to the older literature, the manufacturer of the Hunting series was unknown (Laidacker 1951:115-116; Pollan et al. 1996:47-48; Coysh and Henrywood 1982:296), but recent discoveries indicate that Davenport was quite likely the manufacturer (Arman 1999:7; Earls 2004; Roberts 1998:86,131; Gregg 2006). Indeed, the clinching evidence for Arman was a Hill and Henderson importer's mark on another pattern of the Hunting series. The only other mark on the two Rabbit Hunting plates is on the first (more complete) plate: a stamped "N" (or "Z").

Two red sherds of the pattern Chinese Birds have partial importer's marks of Henderson and Gaines. A very small purple sherd also has a partial Henderson and Gaines importer's mark. The pattern is not known.

The fifth importer's mark is that of Robert Lawrence (or Laurence)[3] of Cincinnati, Ohio (Arman and Arman 1977:100). The (unnamed) view of this red sherd (Figure 1.21) matches that illustrated by Snyder 1997:51) on a 9-inch blue plate; it is one of the series called Florentine Fountain produced by Davenport.[4] As shown in Appen-

---

[3] The two spellings of the surname are given here because the drawing of the importer's mark by Arman and Arman (1977:100) has Laurence, while Cincinnati and genealogical records have Lawrence.

[4] Kolwalsky (1997:7) and Kowalsky and Kowalsky (1999:659) list James & Ralph Clews as the only potter whose wares are known to have been imported by Lawrence, and Arman and Arman (1977:100) state that their Laurence mark is on a Quebec plate in the Cities series by Clews. However, as mentioned earlier, several series

dix 1.1, the date range for the Robert Lawrence ceramics business in Cincinnati was 1830-1835.

Pattern names as given on backstamps are Agricultural Vase, Caledonia, Fountain Scenery (Figure 1.8), Regents Park - The Holme (Figure 1.20 center left), Hoboken in New Jersey, and No. 2 (Figure 1.18). These and other marks are given in Table 1.2.

Figure 1.18 Pattern "No. 2," maker unknown

Figure 1.16 British Scenery series

Figure 1.17 Unknown pattern

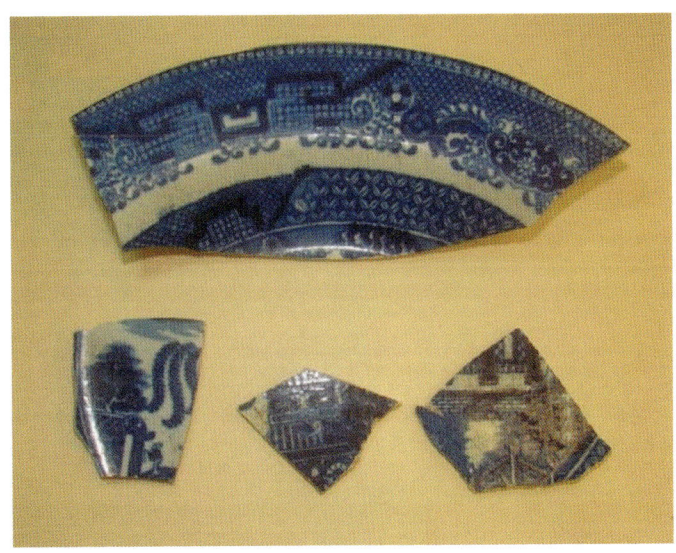

Figure 1.19 Willow pattern

formerly attributed to Clews, including the Cities series, are now known to have been made by Davenport.

Figure 1.20 Transferware series and pattern examples. Left to right, top to bottom: Franklin's Morals series, Amaryllis (2), unknown, Victoria, Regents Park - The Holme, Canova, unknown (2), Fruit & Flowers by Stubbs (2), Palmyra? (2)

Figure 1.21 Robert Lawrence importer's mark (top) on Florentine Fountain series pattern sherd

Flow Blue

Flow Blue is a modified type of transfer decoration in which certain chemicals are added to the glazing compound so that the ink will flow somewhat during the final firing and thus blur the transferware pattern. It was marketed beginning about 1835 and was quite popular through the Victorian era. Blue was the dominant color, but other colors were also used.

Fourteen sherds of flow blue were found at the Powell site. Three are thick rim sherds, with two crossmended; they are probably from a platter about 12.5 inches in length (Figure 1.22). A thinner base sherd has a maker's mark of W Adams & Sons (1829-61) (Furniss et al. 133). The latter four sherds have the pattern Tonquin (Furniss et al. 133; Snyder 1992:57-8; Gaston 1994:131; Williams 1981:54). Another sherd is part of a handle.

There is one sherd of flow black.

Figure 1.22 Flow blue platter, Tonquin pattern by Adams

Slipware

Slipware, sometimes called factory-made slipware, is a term used for slip-decorated fine earthenware that was mass-produced (Sussman 1997: viii). It is often termed dipt, dipped, annular, or banded ware by archeologists and mocha by collectors. The historical name is dipt, where dip according to Rickard (2006:x) was a synonym for slip. Rickard (2006:ix) has a more definitive description of slipware: "factory-made, lathe-turned, refined utilitarian earthenwares whose principal decoration is manipulated slip." Slipware was made from the late eighteenth century on into the twentieth century.

Figure 1.23 Examples of slipware from site 41FB269. Top left: Sherd with mocha decoration. Top center: Sherd with mocha decoration and incised green ring. Bottom: Lid fragment with cat's eye decoration. Right: Carinated bowl with cable decoration and incised blue ring.

There were 51 sherds of slipware found at the Powell site. Examples are shown in Figures 1.23 and 1.24. There is one crossmend cluster of 10 sherds (Figure 1.24) and five crossmend pairs. Thin bands of blue, brown, dark brown, and reddish brown are present, as are wide bands of blue, tan, brown, and greenish gray. Three sherds, including the two upper-left ones in Figure 1.23, have the dendritic decoration known as mocha (Rickard 2006:46-58; Carpentier and Rickard 2001:124-25). Most of the slipware sherds appear to be from bowls.

A lid fragment has cat's eye decoration (Figure 1.23, lower left; see Carpentier and Rickard 2001:126-28). There are four fragmentary bowls with cable decoration (one each in Figures 1.23 right and 1.24; see Carpentier and Rickard 2001:128-30). The cluster in Figure 1.24 has cable decoration on both inside and outside surfaces. Another vessel (not shown), also a bowl, has only ring decoration.

Ten sherds have an incised ring at or near the rim. Two are the top items in Figure 1.23. All these incised rings are colored green, except a blue one at the top right of Figure 1.23. The incising was produced by use of a roulette wheel, and the color was obtained by applying a colored glaze (Sussman 1997:33; Rickard 2006:24).

Five sherds (not shown), one with rouletted green band and all apparently from the same vessel, have a dripped slip decoration in blue, white, and black on a reddish brown slip field (Rickard 2006: Figure 165).

See the section on Yellow Ware for more on slip decoration.

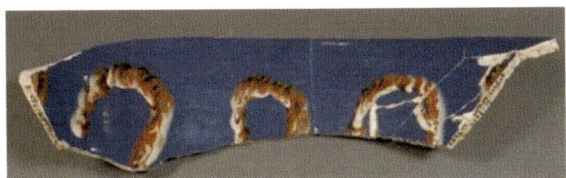 

Figure 1.24 Bowl with cable decoration: interior and exterior

Yellow Ware

Yellow ware is a type of pottery with a yellow-to-buff colored body. It is fired at a temperature of about 1200 C° (2200 F°), then usually a clear alkaline glaze is applied in a second firing. Underglaze decorations such as those discussed for slipware may be applied. The body is usually fairly thick, as in stoneware. However, yellow ware vessels are not vitrified, so a glaze is required for use with liquids. Yellow ware vessels are generally utilitarian: bowls, jugs, pitchers, mugs, chamber pots, and the like.

The yellow ware assemblage found at site 41FB269 consists of 37 sherds, of which seven are decorated. Decorations include blue-colored incised bands, blue and white narrow slip rings, a broad brown slip band, mocha, and molded. The two molded pieces appear to have the same sort of decorative pattern, and to be fragments of round, flat lids. However, the differences in thickness and coloration imply they were not from the same vessel. They were found at disparate locations at the site.

As would be expected, there were no makers' marks or other types of marks on any of the yellow ware sherds. See the section on slipware for more discussion on slip decoration.

Stoneware

A total of 139 sherds of stoneware were recovered. None are very large (as stoneware goes), and only six crossmends were found. Few exhibit the diameter or thickness of a large crockery vessel. None give the appearance of the proverbial gallon jug. There are 28 ginger beer bottle sherds, one impressed "AM RHEIN," and two fragmentary bottle lips. There are various surface colors, including light through dark brown, gray, yellow, and reddish browns. Three sherds appear to be fragments of lids, the top of one being a molded decoration, and another, with a center hole, possibly being from a churn lid. One sherd has a blue appliqué decoration. Eleven small sherds of plain bone china were recovered. No other porcelain was found at the site.

There were no ceramic doll parts, although they have been found at later historic sites in the area.

Other Ceramics

Sixteen fragments of ceramic smoking pipes were found at the site. Seven are from long-stemmed, unglazed, single-unit, white clay pipes (sometimes called kaolin pipes). Of these, five are stem fragments and two are decorated bowl fragments, one a rim and the other a bowl base. The stem diameters range from 5.3 to 7.8 mm and the bore diameters from 2.3 to 2.6 mm.

The other nine items are from two-unit composite pipes, with a bowl and short shank and socket, into which a separate, often non-ceramic, stem was placed (Bradley 2000). One item has an almost complete ribbed shank, with the shank inside diameter going from 7 mm at the tip to 4 mm at the entrance to the bowl. Six other pipe fragments are also decorated, including an effigy bowl. Examples are shown in Figure 1.25.

These pipes are typical of the time period of interest at this site, but there was not enough change in pipe shapes, sizes, decorations, and body constituents during that time period for them to help in the dating of the site.

Figure 1.25 Pipe sherds. Top: white stem, Second row, L to R: bowl base, ribbed stem, bowl fragment, effigy bowl fragment.

Relative Costs of Decorated Tableware and Teaware

During the Powell occupation and beyond to at least 1850, the four popular types of ceramic tableware and teaware (plates, platters, pitchers, tureens, cups, cup plates, saucers, teapots, etc.) were (1) undecorated (called "CC" for cream-colored), (2) edge-decorated, (3) hand-painted, and (4) transfer-printed. Miller (1991) has derived what he calls CC index values, which represent the ratios of prices for various decorated ceramics to those of undecorated (CC) ware. These CC index values vary somewhat with time, vessel type, and vessel size. For shell edge wares, the CC index values for plates (9-10 inches diameter) over the time range of 1824 to 1848 are quite constant around 1.3. For hand-painted wares in the same time period, index values for plates and the smaller-size twifflers (7-8 inches in diameter) are available only for two years, dropping from about 2.2 in 1838 to about 1.7 in 1853. For transferwares, there are indexes for eight years in that period, with plates falling from about 3.2 to about 2.6.

Sussman (1997:51) gives CC index values for transferware, spongeware, and dipped ware (another name for slipware). These are approximately for transferware 2.5, 2.5, 3.0, 2.8, and 2.1 for the years 1824, 1833, 1836, 1846, and 1856, respectively. For spongeware, the values are 1.7, 1.8, 1.9, 1.7, and 1.2. For dipped ware, the values are 1.2, 1.3, 1.4, 1.2, and 1.1.

So, from the high percentage of transferware at the site, it appears that the Powells were using higher priced ceramics for tableware. But this is not extraordinary; archeological excavations and surveys at many sites of this era in this area have yielded predominantly higher priced ceramics, especially transferware.

Observations and Conclusions

From the number of sherds having beginning dates later than 1836, it is surmised that the site was occupied or used as a dump for long after the Powells left. (The archival work by Shelby [2007:19-20] indicates there may have been a successor to the Powell house on the site by 1839.) Nevertheless, the relatively large percentage of deep blue transferware sherds plus a number of sherds of early lighter blue transferware patterns

e.g., those manufactured by Riley and Stubbs, and those formerly identified as manufactured by various Tams partnerships[5]) would tend to indicate the pre-1836 occupation by the Powells. General comparison of the styles and patterns of transferware at this site with those at Velasco (dated 1833-1842 according to Pollan et al. [1996:7]) reveals that the Powell transferware ceramics are, as a whole, decidedly earlier than those at Velasco and Quintana (personal communication with Brazosport Archaeological Society members 2009). Note from the VQ (Velasco-Quintana) column in Table 1.2 that 25 of the 33 non-deep-blue patterns found at the Powell site were also found at Velasco or Quintana, whereas only two of the nine deep blue Powell patterns were at Velasco or Quintana.

The sherds are distributed over much of this large site, and the few areas where they are concentrated appear to be trash pits. So sherd distribution has not been very helpful in the attempt to pinpoint the location of the Powell house. Sherds may have been scattered by the various treasure hunters working at the site over many years, or by earth-grading activities of the owners or lessees. Although the Powell house was burned in 1836, only 49 sherds (2.2%) show evidence of being burned. Perhaps the Powells hid their tableware during the Runaway Scrape or took it with them, or maybe the Mexican Army took it when they left.

There was one trash pit that had many ceramic sherds, a number of them large. Included are most of the sherds with the patterns Rabbit Hunting and Persian (Figures 1.9 and 1.10), plus the 1815-1825 cup plate of the pattern Europa made by Riley (Figure 1.12) and the 1822-1836 cup plate of pattern Game Birds made by Stubbs (Figure 1.14). So this was likely a Powell-era trash pit. This feature was very shallow, only 20 cm, so upper portions may have been removed by earth-grading activities. Nevertheless, the (surviving) layers appeared not to have been disturbed because they contained a number of relatively large, articulated sherds.

---

[5] Until recently, transferware backstamps or impressed marks that include the name Tams were assumed to represent the names of Staffordshire manufacturers, despite the lack of evidence of any such manufacturer. It has now been shown that these were names of Philadelphia ceramics dealers who had imported the ceramics from an undetermined Staffordshire manufacturer (Pomfret 1998; Henrywood 2010).

Another trash pit, of depth 70 cm, yielded the Fountain Scenery transferware pattern plate of Figure 1.8, and another, of depth 25 cm, had by far the most cable-decorated slipware for the site.

There were no sherds with English Registration Marks, which were used 1842-1883 (Godden 1991:526-28). Also there were only a few sherds identified as clobbered or Flow Blue, which post-date the Powell era.

Much more could be said about distribution of ceramics at this site. But, especially because the distribution of pits is so uneven, it is felt that an integrated discussion of the distributions for all the important categories of artifacts for the site would be more appropriate. Perhaps such could be given in a subsequent Journal article.

Acknowledgements

Thanks go to the Brazosport Archaeological Society, especially members Sandra and Johnney Pollan, and Sue Gross for help in identifying a number of patterns via the BAS comparative collection of transferware from Velasco.

GLOSSARY

Cable -- A type of slipware decoration generated by dropping highly overlapped cat's eyes (q.v.) as the slipware vessel is revolved on the lathe and the multi-color slip pot (which forms the cat's eyes) is oscillated longitudinally.

Carinated -- Keel-shaped.

Cat's Eye -- A type of slipware decoration that is circular and composed of three colored segments. It was produced using a three-compartment slip container.

Clobber -- Decoration added to a glazed vessel by application of an enamel.

Cup Plate -- A small plate on which a cup was placed. A portion of tea or coffee was poured from the cup into the saucer to cool down. The cup was then placed on the cup plate to catch spillage or drippings from the cup. The cooled liquid was drunk directly from the saucer. The cup plate is significantly smaller and shallower than the saucer.

London Shape Cup -- A cup which looks like "an inverted truncated cone with a steeply angled shoulder just above a high standing foot ring" (Miller 1991--15). This term is not to be confused with London size cups.

Lustre -- A thin copper or gold decoration added to a white ironstone vessel. It usually consists of a narrow ring around the periphery of the vessel at the lip and, for hollow ware, at the base. One of about 14 types of motifs was often added at one or a few prominent locations on the body.

Mocha Decoration -- Mocha is a type of slipware decoration generated by placing a drop of "tea" on the still-wet slip-covered vessel. The "tea" is a concoction of such components as tobacco juice, stale urine, vinegar, and turpentine. Each drop quickly forms a dendritic pattern (see Figure 1.23). More complex decorations are made by moving the vessel on the lathe and by dragging tools through the initial dendritic patterns. Do not confuse mocha decoration with a coffee-like color referred to as mocha.

Pattern, Series, And View -- For transferware, there are sets of vessels with a common decoration along the border, but different "views" on the rest of the individual vessels. Such a set is called a series and is usually given a name corresponding to the form of the border decoration or to the general subject of the various views in that series. The word "pattern" is a more general term, applying to a series, a view, or the decoration of a vessel that is not part of a series.

Shell Edge -- A form of edgeware decoration that is said to look like the rim of a shell. The design was produced by the mold, and then underglaze blue or green color was applied by hand painting or by dipping the edge of the vessel in paint and rotating it. This is also called feather edge by some collectors.

Slip -- A suspension of clay in water, to which is often added coloring and various substances that modify properties such as adhesion and drying.

Spatterware -- Spatter is decoration applied as a powder or powder mixed with oil, which was then blown on to a vessel. A misconception is that spatter was created dot by dot with a fine brush. However, spatterware, as the term is used by U.S. collectors and in this report, was made mostly by repeated dabbing with an ordinary sponge (Kelly et al. 2001--6-8).

Spongeware -- Decorated ware created by repeated dabbing of paint-soaked root of a sponge. This was essentially a successor to spatterware, the crossover occurring about 1835 (Kelly et al. 2001--6-8).

Stoneware -- Stoneware is made from special clays that do not lose their form when heated to about 1260° C (2300° F). At such a temperature the vessel becomes vitrified and can thus be used without a glaze to store liquids. Nevertheless, a salt glaze was added to most stoneware vessels. Stoneware vessels are generally utilitarian, and most are quite thick and dense. Crockery, jugs, large bowls, ale bottles, and chamber pots were often made of stoneware. The term stoneware was also used in many of the makers' marks of tableware in the latter 1800s. But this was usually on ironstone, not stoneware.

Transferware -- See section on Transferware.

APPENDIX 1.1 Dating of the Robert Lawrence (Laurence) Importer's Mark

As discussed in the section on marks, a sherd with the importer's mark of Robert Lawrence (Laurence) of Cincinnati, Ohio, was found at the site. Very little information on this mark was found in the literature, so an investigation was made to see if a time range for the business could be determined from historical and genealogical information.

Robert Lawrence is listed in the 1830 U.S. Federal Census of Hamilton County, OH, in the second ward of Cincinnati as head of a family with one male aged 40-50, one male 5-10, one female 20-30, and one female 10-15. In the 1831 Cincinnati city directory (Robinson and Fairbank 1831:93), he is listed as a Queensware merchant on Pearl Street north of Main, with home on Longworth between Race and Elm. The same year he is listed in a national directory as a Cincinnati dealer in earthen and China ware, with warehouse in Pearl Street (Jocelyn Darling 1831). In the 1834 Cincinnati city directory (Deming 1834:102,256) he is listed as a Queensware merchant on Pearl Street, and as living at Cincinnati Hotel, located at the northwest corner of Broadway and Front Street. However, he is not listed in the Cincinnati city directories of 1829, 1836, or 1839, nor in the 1840 federal census for Hamilton County, OH. The probate records for Hamilton County (Hamilton County Chapter OGS 1985:321,536,537) show that he was deceased before October 21, 1835, when Thomas N. Williams was appointed administrator of his estate.[6]

On Jan 16, 1837, his widow, Rachel (Williams) Lawrence, was appointed guardian of their four children. Rachel then married a widower, Charles Leeper, and moved farther west (Biographical Publishing Company 1890:727). Thus it appears that the Robert Lawrence (Laurence) importer's mark would have been limited to the years 1830-1835.

It seems remarkable that Coysh (1972:24-5) also states, without reference, that the Florentine Fountain pattern dates from about 1830-1835.[7]

---

[6] Herbert (1993) lists a death notice for a Robert Lawrence in the Cincinnati Daily Gazette of July 8, 1833 with death date July 5. However, the actual newspaper in the archives of the Ohio State Historical Society in Columbus, Ohio, has a simple death notice for Mrs. Robert Lawrence on that date. Even though another Mr. or Mrs. Robert Lawrence was not noticed in other records of this area during this time, we speculate that this indeed was another Mr. or Mrs. Lawrence. Otherwise, the courts would have waited two years to appoint an administrator and three and a half years to appoint the mother as guardian of the children, one of whom, Robert W., was only 11 months old at the time of appointment.

[7] After the above research on Robert Lawrence and family had been completed, there appeared in the TCC Pattern Database (n.d.) a different importer's mark for Robert Lawrence on a plate with the scene Carstairs on the Clyde from the Belle Vue Views series, produced by the Belle Vue Pottery, Hull (1802-1841) (Laidacker 1951:19; Coysh and Henrywood 1982:39). Except for the importer's name, this importer's mark appears to be the same as shown by Arman and Arman (1977:87,101) for the scene Allegheny Scenery, which has the same border as the Belle Vue Views series. The importer in the latter case is Peppard & Callan of Pittsburg. Marje Williams (2006:25-26) reasons (with no reference to Robert Lawrence or Peppard & Callan) that Allegheny Scenery dates from about 1830 to 1834 or a bit later.

Table 1.1 Shapes, Patterns, Lustre Motifs, and Marks
Found on Classical Ironstone at Site 41FB269

Shapes, Patterns, Motifs, Marks	Manufacturer	Dates[1]	Vessel	Diam[2]	Mark No.	References
Shapes						
Laurel Shape	Wedgwood & Co	after 1860	plate	8.5-8.7		Dieringer 100
Lily of the Valley	James Edwards & Son	reg. 1859,61	plate	10.0		Dieringer 105
Mocho Shape	T & R Boote	reg. 1863	mug	3.0		Dieringer 117
Flow Blue Patterns						
Tonquin	Adams					Furniss 133; Snyder 1992:57-8
Copper Lustre Motifs						
Reverse Teaberry	Clementson Bros	1891-1916			KAD B531	Sto 1997:12; 98; Kow 1999:148
Makers' Marks						
BOOTE	T&R Boote	1842-			KAD B276	Kow 1999:116
JAMES /	James Edwards	1842-1854			KAD B837	Kow 1999:182
T.P.C. CO.	Potters Co-Operative Co.	1880s	plate	9.3	KAD A118	Kow 1999:32
The C.C.T.P. CO.	C. C. Thompson	1889-1910			KAD A378	Kow 1999:63
CLEMENTSON BROs ENGLAND	Clementson Bros	1891-1916	saucer	6.0	KAD B531	Kow 1999:148; Godden 1999:214

Notes:

[1] reg. = registered

[2] diameter in inches

Table 1.2 Transferware Patterns Found at Site 41FB269

Series– Pattern -View	Manufacturer	Dates	Colors[1]	Marks	References[2]	VQ[3]	Fig.
Agricultural Vase	RMWear	1836-1858	b, br	"tural"	Wms 1:57, 2:507-9; Sny 2:152	VQ	
Amaryllis	J Heath or RSS		g	"IAL ST"	Wms 1:758, 3:3	VQ	1.21
American Scenery Series	J & J Jackson	1831-1835	b		Sny 1:31, 2:81	VQ	
Asiatic Plants?	W Ridgway, RMWear	ca 1840	p		TCCB 1#1:7,4#1:14;Kow 446,471; Sny2:92	Q	
BAS #50			b	"11"	Pollan 99	VQ	
BAS #76			b		Pollan 103	V	
Bologna	W Adams & Sons	1829-1861	p		Furniss 43; Pollan 21	VQ	
British Scenery	att. J & W Ridgway		b		C&H 1:59-60, 2:35-6;Kow 445, 475		1.18
Caledonia	W Adams	1829-1861	bk	"EDONIA"	Furniss 49-50; Pollan 21	V	
Canova	T Mayer		p,b		Sny 2:124-126	VQ	1.21
Chinese Birds	Davenport	1836-1867	r	impt Henderson &Gaines	Lkt & Gddn #179; C&H 1:325; FOB135:12	V	
Europa	Riley	1802-1828	b	"SemiChina"	Coysh 1:58-9; C&H 1:325		1.12
Florentine Fountain	Davenport	1830-1835	r	"..nci..", impt Robert Laurence, Cincinnati	Arm 2:100; Sny2:51; Gregg 2: Appendix		1.18
Fountain Scenery	W Adams & Sons	1829-1861	b	"Fountain Scenery"	Sny 2:20; Wms 1:265; Furniss 70-1		
French Groups	Davenport	1794-1887	p		Wms 1:40; Pollan 41	V	
Friburg	W Davenport, other	1835-1881	b		Sny2:52; Kow 488	Q	
Franklins Morals	Davenport		db		Ldk 2:39;Camehl 164	VQ	1.21
Fruit & Flowers	Davenport		db		TCCB 8#4:4; Sny 2:99; Arm 4b:23		
Fruit & Flowers	Stubbs	1822-1836	db	"18" imp	Sny2:165		1.21
Game Birds	Stubbs	1822-1836	db		Arm 4b:24		1.14
Gothic	various		bk		Pollan 44; Wms 2:192	V	
Grecian Scenery	several	1822-1854	b		Sny 2:101; Kow 490	VQ	
Hiawatha	Davenport		p		Pollan 46; Wms 3:278; Wms 2:410	V	
Hollyhock	unknown		b		Pollan 46-7; Wms2:30	VQ	
Hunting - Rabbit Hunting	Davenport?	1822-1834	db	"N", impt Hill&Henderson	Gregg 1:19-21; Ldk 2:115-6	V	1.90
London Views -	E Wood & Sons				Sny 2:174-5		
Regents Park-The Holme	E Wood & Sons		db	"EWS/E/ARK"	C&H 1:179, 227; cf. Furniss 79		1.21
Lyre & Vase		ca 1830	bk		Neale 101		
No. 2			r	"No. 2"	cf. Sny 2:175, 7 (No. 107)		1.17
Oriental Villas			b		Pollan 112 (BAS #131)	V	
Palmyra	Furnival?		b		Blake 93	VQ	1.21
Persian	J Heath & Co		b	partial bs, "P"	Wms 2:120; Sny 2:77		1.10
Scott's Illustrations Series	Davenport	1835-1860s	b		Coysh 2:pl.23; C&H 1:324-5	VQ	
Sirius	J & T Edwards		b, r		Sny 2:57	VQ	
Sporting Series-Setter[5]	E Wood & Sons		db		TCCDB; cf. C&H 2:188; Neale 34		1.15
Spread Eagle -	Stubbs	1822-1836	db	"H-- Ne--"	Arm 1:119-125		
Hoboken in New Jersey			db		Arm 1:121-2; Camehl 126-7		
Tams' Foliage -	Tams &		db		Ldk2:83-5; Little Figs.70, 71; C&H 1:356		
Covent Garden Theatre, London			db		C&H 2:63		
Tessino?	J Clementson?	1839-184?	b		Sny 2:46		
Van Dyke	S Alcock	1828-1859	p		Wms 2:260; Pollan 81	V	
Venetian Gardens			b		Wms 1:262	VQ	
Victoria	S Alcock	1828-1859	b	partial bs	Wms 1:53		1.21
Village Church			b		Neale 45; (C&H2:207); Pollan 82-3	V	
Villagers, The	Davenport		b		Sny 2:53		1.11
Virginia	J & R Clews		b		Pollan 84; Wms 2:638	VQ	1.13
Willow			b		C&H1:402-3	VQ	1.20

Notes:

[1] b = blue, bk = black, br = brown, db = deep blue, g = green, p = purple, r = red

[2] TCCB = Transferware Collectors Club Bulletin; TCCDB = Transferware Collectors Club Pattern Database

[3] V = present at Velasco; Q = present at Quintana

References and Other Resources

Arman, David
1999 "The Cities Series and The Don Quixote Series by Davenport—Revisited." *Transferware Collectors Club Bulletin*, Fall 1999, pp.3-5, 7

Arman, David, and Linda Arman
1974 *Historical Staffordshire, An Illustrated Check-List*. Arman Enterprises, Inc., Danville, VA.
1977 *First Supplement Historical Staffordshire, An Illustrated Check-List*. Arman Enterprises, Inc., Danville, VA
2000a *Anglo-American Ceramic Cup Plates - Part I*. Oakland Press, Portsmouth, RI
2000b *Anglo-American Ceramic Cup Plates - Part II*. Oakland Press, Portsmouth, RI

Biographical Publishing Company
1890 *The Portrait and Biographical Album of Fulton County, Illinois*. Chicago

Black, Art, and Cynthia Brandimarte
1987 Henderson & Gaines, New Orleans Ceramics Importers. Research Notes, Historic Sites and Materials, no. 2, Texas Parks and Wildlife Department, Austin, TX

Blake, Marie E., and Martha Doty Freeman
1998 *Nineteenth-Century Transfer-Printed Ceramics from the Texas Coast*. Prewitt and Associates, Inc., Austin, TX

Bradley, Charles S.
2000 "Smoking Pipes for the Archaeologist." In: *Studies in Material Culture Research*, edited by Karlis Karklins, pp. 104-133. The Society for Historical Archaeology

Camehl, Ada Walker
1916 *The Blue China Book*. Halcyon House, New York

Cargill, Diane A., Barbara A. Meissner, Anne A. Fox, and I. Wayne Cox
2004 San Antonio Mission Trails Project, Package 1: Mission Espada (41BX4). Center for Archaeological Research, The University of Texas at San Antonio, Archaeological Survey Report, No. 308, pp. 67-68

Carpentier, Don, and Jonathan Rickard
2001 *Slip Decoration in the Age of Industrialization. In: Ceramics in America* 2001, edited by Robert Hunter. Chipstone Foundation, Hanover and London

Copeland, Robert
1982 *Blue and White Transfer-Printed Pottery*, Shire Album 97, rep 1998. Shire Publications, Princes Risbough, Buckinghamshire, UK
1999 *Spode's Willow Pattern and Other Designs after the Chinese*. 3D ed. Bath Press, Ltd., Bath, UK

Coysh, A. W.
1972 *Blue Printed Earthenware 1800-1850*. David and Charles, Inc., North Pomphret, VT
1974 *Blue and White Transfer Ware 1780-1840*, second revised edition. David and Charles Limited, Newton Abbot, Devon, UK

Coysh, A. W., and R. K. Henrywood
1982 *The Dictionary of Blue and White Printed Pottery 1780-1880*. Antique Collectors' Club Ltd., Woodbridge, Suffolk, UK
1989 *The Dictionary of Blue and White Printed Pottery 1780-1880*, Volume II. Antique Collectors' Club Ltd., Woodbridge, Suffolk, UK

Deming, E.
    1834   *The Cincinnati Directory Advertiser for 1834*. E. Deming pub.

Dieringer, Ernie, and Bev Dieringer
    2001   *White Ironstone China, Plate Identification Guide 1840-1890*. Schiffer Publishing, Ltd., Atglen, PA

Earls, Amy C.
    2004   *Merchant Marks 2*. Henderson Importers of New Orleans (last revised December 21, 2004).
            http://www.greatestjournal.com/community/potterynews/12975.html

Earls, Amy C., Terri L. Myers, Brian S. Shaffer, Karl W. Kibler, Karen M. Gardner, Laurie S. Zimmerman, Elton R. Prewitt, and Sandra L. Hannum
    1996   Testing and Data Recovery at the Townsite of Old Velasco (41BO125), Brazoria County, Texas. Reports of Investigations, Number 94, Prewitt and Associates, Inc., Austin, TX

Fox, Anne A.
    2009   Personal communication

Fox, Anne A., and Kristi M. Ulrich
    2008   *A Guide to Ceramics from Spanish Colonial Sites in Texas*. Special Report #33, Center for Archaeological Research, The University of Texas at San Antonio

Friends of Blue (FOB)
    2007   "Davenport's Chinese Birds," Bulletin 135:12

Furniss, David A., J. Richard Wagner and Judith Wagner
    1999   *Adams Ceramics*. Schiffer Publishing Ltd., Atglen, PA

Gaston, Mary Frank
    1994   *Collector's Encyclopedia of Flow Blue China, Second Series, 131*. Collector Books, Paducah, KY

Godden, Doug
    2009   Enoch Wood's Sporting Series. Friends of Blue Bulletin 142:10

Godden, Geoffrey A.
    1991   *Encyclopaedia of British Pottery and Porcelain Marks*. Barrie & Jenkins, Ltd., London.
    1999   *Godden's Guide to Ironstone Stone and Granite Wares*. Antique Collectors' Club Ltd., Woodbridge, Suffolk, UK

Greer, Georgeanna H.
    1981   *American Stonewares*. Schiffer Publishing Limited, Exton, PA

Gregg, Richard L.
    2006   Evidence from the Elizabeth Powell Site, 41FB269, that the Manufacturer of the Hunting Series of Transfer Printed Pottery was Davenport. Houston Archeological Society Journal 130:19-21

Gross, Sue, and Sandra Pollan
    2009   Personal communication

Halsey, R. T. Haines
    1899   Pictures of Early New York on Dark Blue Staffordshire Pottery. 1974 rep. Dover, New York.

Hamilton County Chapter OGS (pub.)
    1985   Abstract of Book 4 Probate Record 1834-1837. Hamilton County, OH

Henrywood, Dick
    2010   "Tams, Anderson & Tams: A Mystery Solved." Transferware Collectors Club Bulletin 11(1):12-13

Herbert, Jeffrey G.
    1993   Index to Death Notices and Marriage Notices Appearing in the Cincinnati Daily Gazette, 1827-1881, Vol.1

Jocelyn Darling and Co.
    1831   *American Directory for the Year 1831 for Manufactures and Dealers in American Goods.* New York

Kelly, Henry E., and Arnold A. & Dorothy E. Kowalsky
    2001   *Spongeware 1835-1935.* Schiffer Publishing Ltd., Altgen, PA

Kolwalsky [Kowalsky], Arnold
    1997   "Importers, Retailers, Wholesalers, and Auctioneers of Earthenware and Souvenir Wares in the United States and Canada - Part I." China and Glass Quarterly 1(3):7-10

Kowalsky, Arnold A., and Dorothy E. Kowalsky
    1999   *Encyclopedia of Marks on American, English, and European Earthenware, Ironstone, and Stoneware (1780-1980).* Schiffer Publishing Ltd., Artglen, PA

Laidacker, Sam
    1938   *Standard Catalogue of Anglo-American China from 1810 to 1850.* Privately published, Scranton, PA
    1951   *Anglo-American China Part II During the Period from 1815 to 1860.* Privately published, Bristol, PA

Lee, Ruth Webb, and James H. Rose
    1948   *American Glass Cup Plates.* Ruth Webb Lee, Northborough, MA

Little, W. L.
    1969   *Staffordshire Blue.* B. T. Batsford Ltd, London.

Lockett, Terence A., and Geoffrey A. Godden
    1989   *Davenport China, Earthenware, Glass.* Barrie & Jenkins, Ltd., London

McConnell, Kevin
    1990   *Spongeware and Spatterware.* Schiffer Publishing, Ltd., West Chester, PA

Miller, George L.
    1991   "A Revised Set of CC Index Values for Classification and Economic Scaling of English Ceramics from 1787 to 1880. Historical Archaeology" 25#1:1-25
    1995   Blue Shell Edged Plate Classification. Handout at seminar given at Texas Archeological Society Field School, June 11, 1995

Neale, Gillian
    2005   *Encyclopedia of British Transfer-Printed Pottery Patterns* 1790-1930. Miller's, London

Pollan, Sandra D., W. Sue Gross, Amy C. Earls, Johnney T. Pollan, Jr., and James L. Smith
    1996   "Nineteenth-Century Transfer-Printed Ceramics from the Townsite of Old Velasco (41BO125)," Brazoria County, Texas: An Illustrated Catalogue. Prewitt and Associates, Inc., Austin, TX

Pomfret, Roger
    1998   Tams, Anderson & Tams: "A Phantom Factory Revealed—As a Phantom." Northern Ceramic Society Newsletter 112, December

Rickard, Jonathan
    2006   *Mocha and Related Dipped Wares, 1770-1939.* University Press of New England. Lebanon NH

Roberts, Gaye Blake (editor)
    1998   *True Blue, Transfer Printed Earthenware.* Friends of Blue, East Hagbourne, Oxfordshire

Robinson and Fairbank, pub.
    1831   *The Cincinnati Directory for the Year 1831.* Cincinnati

Samford, Patricia M.
    1997   *Response to a Market: Dating English Underglaze Transfer-Printed Wares*, Historical Archaeology 1997 31(2):1-30

Shelby, Robert T.
    2007   Chapter 4, "Historical Summary and Historical Information." In: *The Elizabeth Powell Site (41FB269), Fort Bend County, Texas, Houston Archeological Society Report No. 25, Part 1*, edited by Elizabeth K. Aucoin and Linda L. Swift

Siddall, Judie
    2008   A New Attribution. Transferware Collectors Club Bulletin 8(4):4
    2009   Pointer and Quail. Friends of Blue Bulletin 144:7

Snyder, Jeffrey B.
    1992   Flow *Blue: A Collector's Guide to Pattern, History, and Values*, 57-58. Schiffer Publishing, Ltd., West Chester, PA
    1995   *Historical Staffordshire, American Patriots and Views.* Schiffer Publishing, Ltd., Atglen, PA
    1997   *Romantic Staffordshire Ceramics.* Schiffer Publishing, Ltd., Atglen, PA

Stoltzfus, Dawn, and Jeffrey B. Snyder
    1997   *White Ironstone, A Survey of its Many Forms.* Schiffer Publishing, Ltd., Atglen, PA

Sussman, Lynne
    1997   *Mocha, Banded, Cat's Eye, and Other Factory-Made Slipware.* Studies in Northeast Historical Archaeology, Monograph Series Number 1, Council for Northeast Historical Archaeology

Transferware Collectors Club (TCC)
    n.d.   Transferware Collectors Club Pattern Database. http://transferware.securesites.net/index.html

U.S. Federal Census
    1830   M19 Roll 132, p.42:376

Williams, Margie J.
    2006   *English Pink: American Historical.* Altarfire Publishing, Newcastle, California
    2007   *Collecting English Pink.* Altarfire Publishing, Newcastle, California
    2008   *The Charm of English Pink*, Volume 1, The Pots. Altarfire Publishing, Newcastle, California

Williams, Petra
    1978   *Staffordshire Romantic Transfer Patterns, Cup Plates and Early Victorian China.* Fountain House East, Jeffersontown, KY
    1981   *Flow Blue China, An Aid to Identification*, Revised Edition, 54. Fountain House East, Jeffersontown, KY

Williams, Petra, and Marguerite R. Weber
    1986   *Staffordshire II Romantic Transfer Patterns, Cup Plates and Early Victorian China.* Fountain House East, Jeffersontown, KY
    1998   *Staffordshire III Romantic Transfer Patterns, Cup Plates and Early Victorian China.* Fountain House East, Jeffersontown, KY

Chapter 2
Metal and Miscellaneous Objects

Text and Photographs by Robert T. Shelby

Research finds that there were at least two historical occupancies at site 41FB269 (Elizabeth Powell Site), with no great time-gap between when the first house was burned and a second house was built. It is theorized that the first house was of log construction because of historical context, and the succeeding house was most probably frame construction due to the presence of a great number of nails.

If the items in this section were categorized under a broad heading, most of the artifacts would relate to a household with farm-related activities. Since it has been documented that the site was occupied from about 1830 until probably sometime in the early twentieth century, and the site is in a rural setting, the finding of these types of objects was no great surprise to the investigators.

Metal objects were a great portion of the artifacts recovered from the Powell site. This was true of the findings from the test pits and from the metal detector survey (MDS). A total weight of 76.5 pounds of metal objects was brought to the lab. After cleaning and weighing, it was determined that 54.5 pounds were objects deteriorated beyond recognition, leaving 22 pounds of metal artifacts to document. This total does not include nails, metal buttons, coins, and firearm related items.

The following sections of the report describe the remainder of the metal artifacts that are in some recognizable form. This includes objects of several types of metal. Also, let it be noted that some items do not fit into neat categories and therefore may not be metal, but are kept in this portion of the report for lack of any other proper place. The only metal artifacts in this section of the report to be excluded are nails, coins, and buttons, which were documented in the Houston Archeological Society publication *The Elizabeth Powell Site (41FB269) Report 25, Part 2*, and

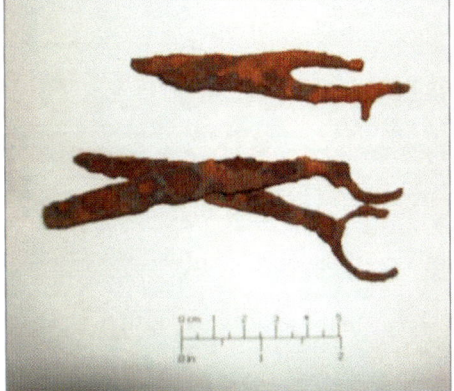

Figure 2.1 Scissors

firearms and related items, which are in another section of the present volume (Part 3) of the report.

All of the metal artifacts from this site were in some stage of degeneration, especially the ferrous objects. Therefore, most measurements given in this report are approximate due to the rusted condition of these artifacts. Also, the measurements are given in English inch scale as this was the system in use when most of the products were made.

For purposes of description, the artifacts are allotted to the following groups: (1) **personal objects**, (2) **interior household**, (3) **exterior and farm related**, and (4) **miscellaneous** (items not included in the other categories).

Personal Objects

There was a time when practically every man and boy in North America carried a pocketknife, if for no other reason than to whittle, a pastime greatly favored in early Texas. It would also have been especially useful in daily chores on a farm. The specimen found at in Pit F, level 16, at the Powell site is about 3 inches long, about ½ inch wide and approximately 3/8 inch thick, including the bone scales that form the handle and the very rusted inner parts. It has no bolsters. The bone scales are attached on either side by two brass rivets, one slightly larger and below the other, and three small steel/iron pins near the bottom. The knife blade was in a closed position at the time of deposition. It is difficult to tell if the knife had more than one blade as the inner metal scales and the blade have rusted together. The bone and the metal are in an advanced stage of deterioration (cat. no. 248).

Found together in Pit AM, level 3, were two small pairs of scissors. Although highly rusted with some pieces missing, one pair remains somewhat intact and is in better condition to study. When new, both pairs were about five inches in length. These were probably ladies' sewing scissors, the small type used in embroidery. Their deteriorated condition doesn't allow any maker's marks or any other identifying signs to be observed (cat. no. 1083, Figure 2.1). A similar set of scissors was recovered at an 1836 Mexican Army campsite in Wharton County (see HAS Report No. 13, Figure 52).

Two parts of a non-ferrous metal spur (probably brass) were found in Pit AI. The smaller piece (spur strap box) was found in level 3 and the larger part of the spur (shank and arms), except for the rowel that is missing, was found in level 4. The spur was about 2¼ to 2½ inches from arm to arm, before one arm was bent askew, probably during the depositional process. Together the pieces weigh

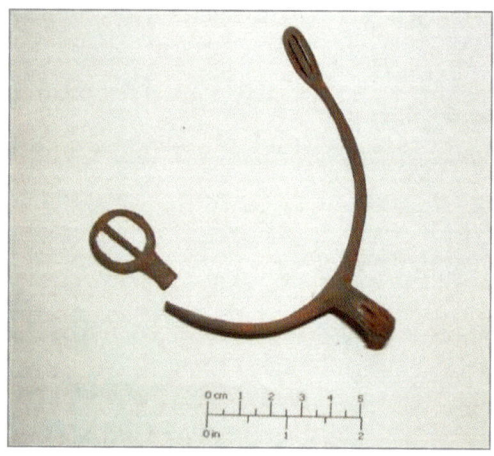

Figure 2.2 Spur fragments

41.9 grams. R. Stephen Dorsey, author of *The American Military Spur*, features a similar spur in his book and says it was a non-governmental issue military style spur, probably privately purchased for militia use, and dates from the Late Indian War period (circa 1812 to 1821). The spurs of that time period were largely handmade, and as there was no standardization of these privately purchased spurs, the specimen from Pit AI isn't an exact duplicate of the Dorsey illustration. There are no stampings or maker's marks on the spur. One scenario is that this spur's presence at the Powell site suggests that it could have been lost by an Anglo Texian who

had been in a militia unit back in the United States (cat.nos.137 and 1145, Figure 2.2).

Also in Pit AI, level 3, was a small shirt stud or collar button. This decorative item is made of bronze or brass with a scalloped motif set off in the center with a tiny faceted red stone. The item measures 5/16 inch from the top of the stone in front to the metal button in

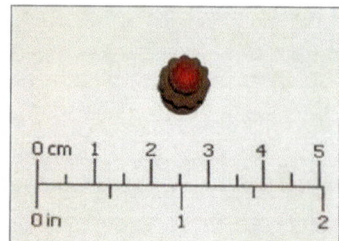

Figure 2.3 Shirt or collar button

the rear and is about 5/16 inch at its greatest diameter. It is a one piece type shirt fastener and doesn't have to be taken apart to use. No maker's mark was found (cat.no.138, Figure 2.3).

What appears to be a small decorative hair clip is from Pit W, level 4. It is formed from a small strip of copper, bent double back onto itself with the two ends now together, to form a spring-like clip. At each end is a small thin piece of copper stamped in the form of a stylized fan of 11 feathers. The end pieces have broken off. The back of the end pieces are stamped with a web or screen-like design. No other marks are on the piece to identify the maker (cat. no. 269).

Interior Household

Found in level 3 of Pit BD is a brass object identified as a partial candleholder, about three inches long and lacking its base. The tube that houses a candle has an exterior diameter of ¾ inch and is decorated in various areas on the length of the tube with lightly inscribed rings. The small lever that extended through a slot in the side of the tube, normally used to raise and lower the candle, is missing. The drip pan that surrounds the top of the

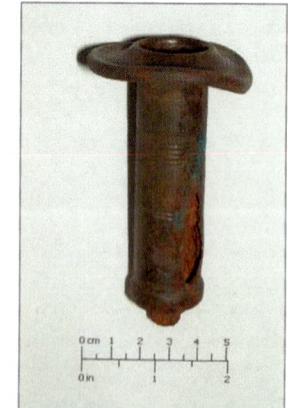

Figure 2.4 Partial candleholder

holder is slightly deformed, but is about 2 inches in diameter. The tube has a rigid object stuck inside to about ¾ of its length. A non-ferrous metal, rod-like object, about 3/8 inch long and 3/8 inch in diameter, protrudes from the bottom of the tube and possibly had some function in attaching the missing base. Gregg Dimmick, following the trail of the retreating Mexican army, found a similar, better-preserved candleholder. He illustrates it in his book, *Sea of Mud,* on page 243, stating that the similarities of the two candleholders led him to believe the one he found might have come from Mrs. Powell's. No maker's mark was found (cat. no. 1314, Figure 2.5).

A small rosette with a pull ring of twisted wire was found in Pit Z, level 14. The rosette is stamped from very thin copper, about 15/16 inch in diameter, and appears to have been painted with gold paint. About ¼ of the rosette is missing. The pull

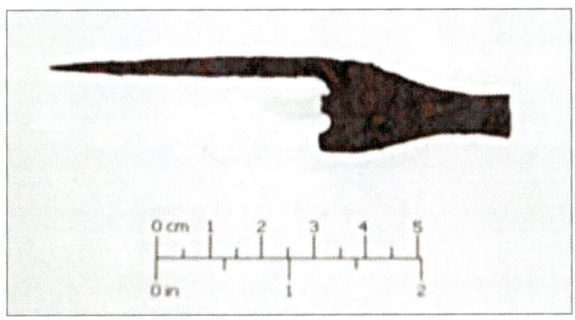

Figure 2.5 Fork fragment

ring is made of a similar material and attaches through a hole in the center of the rosette. Finely made, this artifact was probably from a shop that specialized in crafting such objects, although it bears no maker's marks. It possibly was on a tray or drawer to a small box, although there is no indication of how it could be fastened (cat. no. 801).

Pit M5, level 4, yielded an iron or steel fork. The fork is missing most of its handle and two of its three tines. It is about ¾ inch across the area where the tines would join. Like most of the ferrous material at this site, the fork was found in a highly rusted condition. No maker's

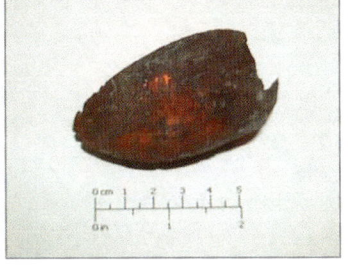

Figure 2.6 Bowl of a spoon

marks were found (cat. no. 2215, Figure 2.5).

Another table utensil found at the site was from Pit T, level 8 and was the bowl part of a serving-type spoon. It was made of copper and coated with silver and is missing a handle. In cleaning the hard-caked mud from this object, the silver began to disappear, so complete cleaning was stopped. The spoon bowl is 2 ¾ inches in length along the curvature of the bottom and about 1 ¾ inches along the curvature of the width of the spoon bottom at its widest point. No stamping or other marks could be found on the spoon (cat. no. 1478, Figure 2.6).

Pit CA, level 3, yielded a flat iron (old type sad iron), 5 3/8 inches long by 3 1/2 inches wide near the base end. In its present condition, which is highly rusted and missing a handle or grip, it weighs 1205.5 grams or slightly over 2 1/2 pounds. Except for the distinctive clothes iron shape it would be difficult to identify this artifact as it has no manufacturing marks. There were a number of

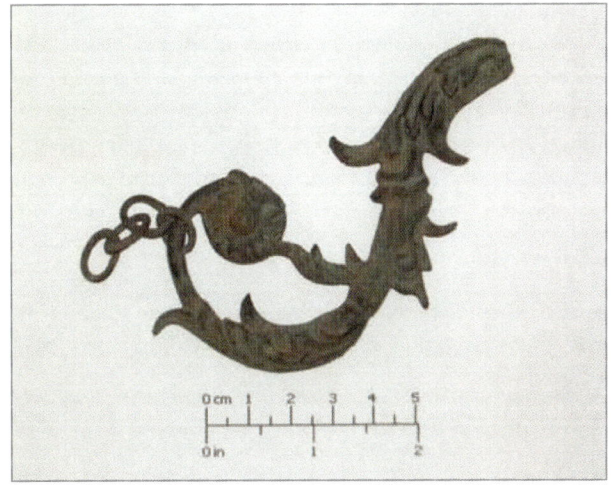

Figure 2.7 Bronze fragment

these irons on the surface at the site when the archeological testing began. However, before they could be taken to the lab for study, they had disappeared (cat. no. 2026).

A bronze, highly decorated piece, probably broken off a hanging lamp, was in Pit AA, level 3. The item is hard to measure as it is in the form of a shepherd's crook when viewed from one perspective. A rough measure would make it about four and one-quarter inches long by about two inches at its widest section. It is cast with a design that resembles a leafy vine. Four small links of bronze chain hang from the bend in the "crook." The lamp to which this piece was originally attached was probably fairly large. No maker's marks are present (cat. no. 1167, Figure 2.7).

The metal detector survey at location MDS 46 found a small brass pull-knob of the type often used on cabinets in houses. It is 5/8 inch from front to rear and ¾ inch in diameter at the round part of the front of the knob. It has what appear to be the remnants of a rusted screw in the base end where the knob attaches to the cabinet door. There are no maker's marks (cat. no. 2773).

A kerosene lantern wick shield was found in Pit C, level 3, and still retained some soot around the opening where the wick protruded and would have held the flame. The object is made of brass and is about 1 ½ inches in diameter and has a vertical profile of about 1 inch. The object is generally cup-shaped with a slit made in the dome portion to allow the wick to protrude. No maker's marks were found (cat. no. 277).

The metal detector survey found a stove lid lifter. It is designated MDS Surface. It is cast iron, about 8 ¾ inches in length. It is made from a bar of metal, 5/8 inch square. There is a slot in one end, probably to allow the tool to be hung up when not in use. At the other end is an abrupt bend that tapers to a blunt point. This bend and point were what enabled the device to lift lids that had slots or rings. The lids covered wood-burning cast iron stoves. No maker's marks were found (cat. no. 2215).

In Pit D, level 1, was an iron drawer pull. It is shaped like the letter C with the opening between the arms of the C about 2 3/8 inches. It is formed from round iron rod about ¼ inch diameter (cat. no. 995).

Pit AU, level 4, also had a drawer pull but of a larger size. The opening for the hand grip is about 2 ½ inches. It is formed from 3/8 inch round iron stock. This level also contained a 3 inch rivet with washer still attached (cat. no. 2631).

Pit L, level 5, yielded a steel bottle cap known as a crown type that was made for soft drink and beer bottles. It has a plastic insert below the metal cap and this means that it was produced sometime after 1960. The metal cap is too rusted for the brand name to be readable (cat. no. 668).

Exterior and Farm Related

A shingling ax is a specialized combination tool used for splitting and nailing wood shingles on a roof. The major parts are a handle, usually of wood about a foot long, rounded to hold easily in one hand, and an iron or steel head attached to one end of the handle. The head has an ax bit on one side and a hammer on the other. However, all that remains of the shingling ax found in Pit U, level 3, is the head with the hammer. The ax bit appears to be broken off and no portion of the wood handle remains. The nose end of the hammer is battered and mushroomed near the end as though the tool had been used to beat something harder than nails (cat. no. 440).

An auger 10 ½ inches in length, for boring a ½ inch hole and made of iron or steel, was removed from Pit V, level 5. The helical end is only three inches of the total length of the shaft and the part that would have the lead screw and the flukes or spurs is missing. The long shank is slightly bent near the tail end. The shank is square, not round, indicating this bit was made to fit a twist brace rather than the more modern iron brace. However, the last inch has been flattened, indicating that it might also have been adapted to use with a wooden cross handle. An unknown black substance is present, adhering to the flats of the spiral and in places along the shank (cat. no.816).

Pit AI, level 3, also had an auger, or at least 4 ½ inches of the broken end of what was a double twist auger bit, made to create a 1 5/8 inch hole. The helical or twist end is roughly broken off from the rest of the tool, which is missing, and the lead screw from the tip is also missing. This iron or steel tool is rusted yet the spurs/flukes are fairly sharp (cat.no.1061).

In Pit AO, level 3, a small rusted drill bit four inches long and ¼ inch in diameter was recovered. The helical portion is about 1-¼ inches. The tail end of the shank is flattened to fit into a cross handle. The item is bent about half the length of the shank to about a 90-degree angle. This bit has a small lead screw at the tip. It has no spurs and is a twist drill bit known as a gimlet. Its most common function was to make small holes in wood for starting screws (cat. no. 2618).

The most common method of nailing and supporting a wire fence is the use of staples. A fence staple is a U-shaped fastener usually made of iron or steel, formed into a wire, and cut off at certain lengths and then each piece is bent to the U shape. The tips of each end of the arms of the U are sharpened to allow the staple to be driven into a wooden fence post. Staples were recovered from Pits AC (1), AE (3), AX (1), BF (1), O (2), V (1), and W (1). These 10 staples ranged from 1 ¼ to 1-¾ inches in length. If soil conditions at the site were better for preservation of ferrous material, many more staples would probably have been found. The presence of even this limited number of staples indicates that there were wire fences at the site and that these fences were most likely for animal control (cat. nos. 406, 484, 339, 2666, 1631, 742, 869, 821, and 1534).

Three horseshoes were recovered from three separate pits. The metal shoes from Pit T, level 8 and Pit BH, level 1 were fairly intact although rusted to a great degree. The shoe from Pit BH still has a nail clinched over it. This might mean that it was a "thrown" shoe, rather than a discarded shoe. Pit M5, level 3, had a horseshoe rusted so badly that only about ¾ of the original was left (cat. nos. 1478, 982, and 2207).

Horse harnesses have a number of buckles to aid in adjusting the harness to each individual animal. Pit M1, level 2 had a rusty buckle with rounded front edges that was probably a harness buckle. MDS 10 found a larger item that greatly resembles a buckle, although its advanced state of deterioration makes that hard to confirm (cat. nos.1545 and 2735).

Several other horse harness attachments were recovered, including a hame trimming ring from Pit M1, level 3, a small D-ring from Pit B, level 3, and a halter D-ring from Pit AA, level 2, and a D-buckle from Pit BH, level 7, (cat. nos. 1103, 169, 906, and 905).

A singletree/whiffletree center clip was recovered by metal detector and recorded as MDS 15. The object is made of cast iron and fits astride the middle of a singletree to allow fastening something such as a buggy, wagon, or plow to a horse. The clip is 3 3/8 inches in one direction and about 2 inches across the shroud-like portion that fits on the singletree. From this shroud a ring extends to accept a ring attached to the harness rigging. No markings of any kind are evident on the piece which was brought to the lab in a very rusted condition (cat. no. 2739).

Pit CA, levels 3 and 5, each revealed a side board stake bracket which is also used as a wagon bow staple. These objects were used to hold boards on wagon sides or bows that go across the wagon to hold up a cover. Both brackets are made of iron straps and formed in the general shape of a flattened letter C, with extensions at the top and bottom. There is a hole at each end to allow the device to be riveted to the conveyance. From hole to hole, one bracket is 3 3/8 inches. The other, larger, bracket is 3 5/8 inches between holes. Both pieces are ¾ inch wide and made from 1/8 inch thick metal. The pocket formed by the bend of each would accept a board of ½ inch thickness. They have a slight bevel along the length of each exterior side. Although there are no manufacturer's marks, these brackets appear to be factory made (cat. nos. 2011 and 2034).

Another type of wagon bow staple was found by metal detector and designated MDS 62. This object is shaped like a staple in that it is shaped like the letter U with the tips of the arms of the U sharpened in order to nail the staple into the side of a wagon or buggy. The staple then holds the bows that support a top or cover over the vehicle. The object is iron or steel and is about two inches across the open throat. It is too rusted to have any maker's marks extant (cat. no. MDS 62).

Figure 2.8 Rectangular brass object

Two 1 ¾ inch chain links were recorded, one from the cistern, the single feature at the site at level 12. The other link was from Pit M4, level 3, (cat. nos. 1835 and 2251).

Miscellaneous

Pit M1, level 5, had an interesting brass object resembling a belt buckle more than anything else. It is 2½ inches long by 11/16 inch wide by 1/16 inch in thickness. This rectangular object has corners that are clipped in an indented curvature. One face is smooth and finished and will be called the front. The front has no markings or signs that anything had ever been attached. The apparent rear side is not as finely finished and has four prongs about ¾ inch in length and about 1/8 inch average diameter, located one at each corner. Several of the prongs are bent over as though they had been used to attach this item to something else. It has been suggested this item is similar to the buckles used on the cross-the-chest belts worn by Mexican troops, although no match has been located in illustrations of the period (cat. no. 1260, Figure 2.8).

Pit S, level 8, yielded an as yet unidentifiable object, a brass or bronze tube, open at both ends, 3 3/4 inches long and 1 ¼ inches at its greatest diameter, the wall of the tube being approximately 1/16 thick. The object, when not viewed from the end and only the length showing, resembles a lath turning with rounds and indentions. The object is, however, a casting. A small rectangular section is cut out from a lip on one end. There are lines incised around the tube in several places. It has been suggested this object is a portion of a candlestick. There are no maker's marks (cat. no. 1328).

From Pit M3, level 3, is one of those objects that defy classification since it hasn't been identified. The object is made from brass about 1/32 inch thick and is black, either from paint or some other application. It is 2 3/8 inches long and about ¾ inch wide. It is hard to give precise measurements of this object because of its shape. From what might be called its front, it is incised with various lines. The middle of the piece has an inscribed oval; above that is a fan-like design. The lower end tapers to a rounded point. The object is bent and curves slightly to the rear. The reverse has a stud about 5/16 inch long by 5/16 inch diameter. The piece is elegant, yet not precisely made, as if created by hand rather than by machine. It has no maker's marks (cat. no. 2166, Figure 2.9)

Another curious object made of brass and weighing 100 grams was found in Pit B, level 2. The object is round, 3 7/8 inches in outer diameter.

It has an inner ring or hole, 1 13/16 inches in diameter. The object's profile height is 7/16 inch. There are 16-3/16 inch round holes equally spaced along the outer perimeter. The object is a well machined piece with two small ear-like pieces that rise above the profile. One ear has a small pin pointing inward into the groove or track between the inner hole and the outer ring with the 16 holes. Opposite the ear with the pin on the other side of the track is another ear that has a hole threaded as if to accept a screw. The impression is that the pin and possible screw were to hold something upright that rested in the track. The general consensus is that this object is the base to a lamp or lantern and that a glass chimney fit in the

Figure 2.9 Unidentified Object

track, although no illustration has been found to match. There are no maker's or other identifying marks (cat. no.134).

The following chart is a continuation of the description of the metal and miscellaneous artifacts in an abbreviated form. Artifacts discussed in the text are not included in the chart.

Table 2: Metal and Miscellaneous Objects

Cat.	Pit	Level	Item
169	B	3	Wire bail (bucket handle).
2688	EC	3	Wire bail (bucket handle).
2692	EC	3	Iron, donut shape, flat both sides – 2″ dia. x 5/8″ thick.
787	Y	3	Circular pc. lead, ½″ dia., suggested as gaming piece.
1413	E	3	Small horseshoe shape, iron, suggested boot heel insert.
1166	AA	3	9″ iron spike.
626	F	4	9½″ x ½″ sq. iron bar, one end pointed, one flat & bent.
405	G	3	10″ x ½″ sq. iron bar, one end like nail head, other cut.
1774	BG	3	Bronze thumb screw, small, full- no ears, no markings.
189	BA	2	Brass thumb screw, small, with ears, no markings.
981	BH	1	1 3/8 ″ iron slot-head wood screw.
117	A	3	5″ long fancy head iron bolt with 7/8″ sq. nut rusted on.
1684	Y	1	¾″ iron square nut.
2670	AX	4	a)1″ iron slot- head wood screw. b) ½″ sq. head bolt c) 2 3/8″ rivet w/ lg. head. d)1 ¼″ rivet w/ pc. metal.
2148	M3	3	1 3/8″ iron rivet.
1665	AK	5	1 3/8″ iron rivet.
1245	AK	2	2 3/8″ iron rivet or bolt. Badly rusted.
2273	CB	4	3″ iron bolt w/ washer rusted on.
1597	M1	2	Copper rivet, size similar to ones in Levi pants.
1168	AA	3	Small copper wire w/ loop twisted in one end.
2041	CA	5	Small, flat copper strip w/ small copper pin inserted.
2083	M6	3	Clothing hook and eye, copper. Probably not a pair.
1427	DA	1	2 brass items: one flat- round w/hole in center; one sm. pc.- flat w/ hole, missing parts.
1841	Cist.	12	2 flat pcs. brass, one highly decorative; no markings.
1314	BD	3	Brass or copper – flared one end , no maker's marks.
953	BH	7	1 ¼″ dia. iron dome/cap-like object w/ hole in center.
1597	M1	2	Sm. copper tube w/ fin-like attachment. Part of mach.
1033	BH	14	1″ copper, round w/ fin-like extensions-center hole.
1320	T	1	Circular brass, flat, 2 ¼″ dia., open w/ connections.
1064	AI	3	Brass ring ½″ dia., similar to small washer or "O" ring.
1453	T	6	Highly rusted iron cap, app. 4 ¼″ dia. No marking.
2411	AH	5	Iron, 2 ¼″ x 1 ¼″ w/ diamond hole.
2769	MDS	#42	Same as above.
481	AE	2	Small nickel-plated steel alligator clip (elect. connector).
1009	BB	2	Possible steel knife handle minus grips or blade.
1791	AQ	4	Possible steel knife handle w/ 2 rivets, no grips or blade.
2346	AS	2	Small half – flat ring w/ holes spaced evenly, brass.

Table 2 (continued)

1931	CA	7	Lead object w/ rusted iron attached at end by rivet.
2733	MDS	#4	Bent rod w/ attached "head" w/ set screw
431	H	2	Iron fitting w/holes to fasten the object. Has hook at end.
13	AA	2	Small spike w/mushroomed head. Shank bent in "L" shape.
905	BH	7	¼″ iron rod bent into out-of-round ring.
2745	MDS	#20	Partial machine-cut nail. Retrieved after nail report.
1906	CB	5	Thin iron round cap, approx. 1¼″ dia. No markings.
2227	M5	6	Thin iron octagonal item. Approx. 1¼″ dia. No markings.
2151	M3	3	Iron wire, app. 8″ long.
2165	AU	5	Broken iron strap adjuster/ buckle.
1569	AK	3	Misc. iron washer and springs.
2608	AJ	4	Flat, non-ferrous object, 1/8″ thick x 4″ at greatest dim.
2651	AN	3	Iron ring broken from some other object.
1223	AK	Sur.	Iron buckle? No markings, badly rusted.
1689	AA	2	Brass decorative tack head. Pin part missing.
2586	AP	3	Same as above, with two point type fastener.
2421	AS	3	Same, partial pin still in place.
1723	M1	2	Same as above.
1689	AA	2	Same, point missing.
2586	AP	3	Same, Two point fastener.
2683	EC	1	Same as above, one point.
2438	AJ	2	Same as above.
1688	M2	1	Same as above.
1064	AI	2	Two tacks, same as above.
1760	BF	3	Small flat piece of lead.
474	U	2	Iron strap and flat piece of iron. This and following are probably part of wood burning stove. No marking.
2463	AJ	2	Similar to above.
2736	MDS	#12	Iron plate app. 2″ x 3″ with protrusions. No markings.
416	AE	2	Misc. iron broken from larger item, possibly stove.
2801	MDS	#73	Iron piece shaped like small propeller w/ hole as for mount on shaft. Approx. 8″ in length. Badly rusted. No marks. Probably broken from larger iron object.
332	E	6	¾″ x 1¼″ iron bar, rectangular in cross section. Approx. 7″ in length.
985	BH	1	Iron item w/hole at one end, possibly part of hinge.
1931	CA	7	Object like small pick-ax head. One end lead, opposite end of head-iron & rusted badly. Two ends attached by rivet in middle. No markings.

The foregoing metal artifacts represent those objects that are describable and recognizable or partially describable and not so recognizable. The ground conditions at Site 41FB269 are not favorable for the preservation of ferrous material, and much of what was recovered was rusted, sometimes to the point of mere lumps or red dust.

The metal artifacts described in this report are largely domestic or agricultural, and this agrees with the known history of the site: that of farmhouses in a rural and agricultural setting. People lived in these houses and pursued farming and animal husbandry as did a large portion of Americans in the nineteenth and early twentieth centuries.

References and Other Resources

Bounty Books
    1986   *Sears, Roebuck Catalogue, 1902 Edition.* Reprint. New York, NY. Distributed by Crown Publishers, Inc.

DBI Books
    1970   *Sears, Roebuck and Co. Consumers Guide, Fall 1900.* Chicago, Ill. Reprint. Northfield, IL

Digest Books, Inc
    1971   *Sears, Roebuck Catalogue, 1908.* Replica edition. Northfield, IL

Dimmick, Gregg J.
    2004   *Sea of Mud.* Austin, Texas. Texas State Historical Association

Dorsey, R. Stephen
    2000   *The American Military Spur.* Eugene, Ore. Collectors' Library

Dover Publications, Inc.
    1969   *Montgomery Ward Catalogue No. 57. Spring and Summer 1895.* Reprint. New York, NY

Elkhart Manufacturing Company
    2001   *Horse-Drawn Carriage Catalog 1909.* Elkhart, Ind. 1909. Reprint. Dover Publications. Mineola, NY

Hudgins, Joe D. and G. Dimmick
    1998   *A Campsite of the Retreating Mexican Army, April, 1836, 41WH91, Wharton County, Texas.* Houston Archeological Society Report No. 13

Ventura Books, Inc.
    1979   *Sears, Roebuck and Co., Consumer Guide, Fall 1909.* Chicago, Ill. Reprint. New York, NY

Chapter 3
Munitions Artifacts
Text, Maps and Illustrations by Thomas L. Nuckols
Photography by Linda L. Swift

Introduction

This chapter will detail the 69 munitions artifacts recovered at the Elizabeth Powell site. The artifacts are divided into the following categories: spherical muzzle-loading lead bullets, an unidentified spherical muzzle-loading lead bullet, lead sprues, gun flints, lead shot, lead buckshot, percussion caps, percussion revolver lead bullets, rimfire cartridge cases, center-fire cartridge cases, lead cartridge bullets, a shotshell, gun parts, and a powder charge measure. Maps are included that show the distribution of the munitions artifacts. Maps, detailed tables and illustrations, as well as a glossary can be found at the end of the chapter, following notes and references. Figure and illustration numbers are keyed to the tables.

Maps

Artifact distribution maps are provided which show all of the units excavated at the site[1], as well as metal detector hits that yielded munitions artifacts. Not all of the units contained munitions artifacts. Only the metal detector/shovel tests that yielded munitions artifacts are depicted. The munitions artifacts are divided into three categories. Each of the sub-categories is represented by a symbol. Single artifacts shown on the maps are depicted by one of three symbols. These symbols are:

● Artifact probably dating to the time of the Powell occupation (Spherical muzzle-loading lead bullet, unidentified spherical muzzle-loading lead bullet, lead sprue, gun flint, gun parts and the powder charge measure).

+ Artifact dating to the post-Powell occupation (percussion cap, percussion revolver lead bullet, rimfire cartridge case, center-fire cartridge case and lead cartridge bullets).

✕ Artifact questionable as dating to the Powell or post- Powell occupation (lead shot and some of the lead buckshot).

<u>Artifacts</u>

Spherical Muzzle-loading Lead Bullets

Six spherical muzzle-loading lead bullets were recovered at the site (Figure 3.1, Table 3.1).

Figure 3.1 Spherical Muzzle-Loading Lead Bullets

Four of the six bullets were fired. Four bullets show evidence of being cast in bullet molds (Illustration 3.1). The six bullets probably date to the time of the Powell occupation of the site. The bullets are too small (0.50" diameter or less) for military ammunition[2]. They are, however, the right size for bullets used during the Colonial era of Texas. At that time, the two most common types of firearms were the Kentucky rifle[3] and pistol. These guns were never mass produced, but were the individual creation of small shops or individual gunsmiths. While each maker often had his own preferences, guns were often made to a customer's specifications. The purchase of a new rifle included a bullet mold of the proper size (Nonte 1973: 145, Worman 2007: 18). Before the development of standardized calibers, the size of a Kentucky rifle or pistol bullet was referred to as "so many balls to the pound" (Dillin 1967: 83). To make loading easier, bullets were smaller than the bore of these guns. For the rifling to be effective, bullets had to be wrapped in a greased leather or cloth patch. Since the bullet did not contact the rifling, fired bullets do not exhibit rifling imprints (Illustration 3.2).

Unidentified Spherical Muzzle-loading Lead Bullet

An unfired spherical lead bullet with the sprue attached and a mold seam was found on the site (Figure 3.2, Table 3.2). It was probably cast in a worn mold which gave it a slight elliptical shape of approximately 0.608"Ø[4] X 0.616" long. These dimensions are too small for a musket ball and too large for a rifle or pistol bullet. It is possible that this bullet was intended for a Baker rifle or a Paget carbine, British made weapons used by the Mexican Army[5]. These guns used a bullet diameter of approximately 0.620".

Figure 3.2 Unidentified Spherical Muzzle-loading Lead Bullet

Lead Sprues

Evidence that lead bullets were cast on the site is represented by four sprues (Figure 3.3, Table 3.3). A sprue is a piece of excess lead (often "mushroom" shaped with a cap and stem) that is attached to a bullet where the molten lead is poured into a

Figure 3.3 Lead Sprues

bullet mold. The sprue is cut off the bullet with the mold's integral sprue cutter (see Illustration 3.1). A sprue is either discarded or saved and used to cast more bullets.

Gun Flints

Seven unifacially worked gun flints were excavated at 41FB269 (Figure 3.4, Table 3.4). Gun flints were used in muzzle-loading firearms equipped with a flintlock ignition system (Illustration 3.4). Flint-

Figure 3.4 Gun Flints

lock firearms were in use from around 1625 through the first half of the 19th century. The percussion cap ignition system replaced the flintlock.

Lead Shot and Lead Buckshot

One lead shot and fifteen lead buckshot were found at the site (Tables 3.5 and 3.6). Four of the buckshot show evidence of mold casting. Shot and buckshot are a type of ammunition that shoots out

in all directions and is based on the theory that some of it will probably hit the intended target. In the earliest days of firearms, when all guns were smooth-bored, shot referred to any projectile regardless of size and without differentiation as to number of projectiles fired simultaneously. With the advent of rifling, the term "bullet" replaced shot in reference to single projectiles fired through a rifled barrel (Nonte 1973: 22). Eventually, the term shot came to signify small lead pellets (0.04"Ø to 0.23"Ø) used to hunt birds and small game. Larger lead pellets (0.24"Ø to 0.36"Ø) used for hunting bigger game such as deer became known as buckshot. Shot and buckshot were used in muzzle-loading muskets[6], muzzle-loading shotguns and shotshells. At the time of the Powell occupation of the site, shot and buckshot were made in molds or shot towers. In 1789, a patent was granted to a British plumber from Bristol named William Watts. Watts discovered a technique for making shot that was perfectly globular in form, without the dimples, scratches, imperfections and non-aerodynamic seam which other shot heretofore manufactured usually have on their surface (Minchinton 1990). Watts knocked out holes in the floors of his three story house and placed a water tank on the first floor. On the top floor, Watts poured molten lead into a sieve. The falling lead formed into spheres and solidified when it hit the water in the tank. Watts' home became the first shot tower, and it was so successful that shot towers were erected all over England and Europe. The United States relied almost exclusively on imported shot. In 1807, President Thomas Jefferson imposed the Embargo Act[7], ending the shot supply from abroad. Shortly thereafter, shot towers were built in the United States.[8] Today, most shot and buckshot are machine-made; however, there are some shot towers still operating in the United States[9].

Percussion Caps

Two copper percussion caps were recovered (Figure 3.7, Table 3.7). A percussion cap is a small copper cup containing fulminate of mercury, a detonating

Figure 3.7 Percussion Caps

compound which explodes when it is struck. Percussion caps were a form of ignition for percussion lock equipped muzzle-loading firearms and percussion revolvers. The percussion cap is placed over a nipple and is struck by the hammer which crushes the detonating compound against the nipple, igniting it, and causing a jet of flame to ignite the main powder charge. (Nonte 1973: 188) (Illustration 3.7). Credit for the invention of the percussion cap is somewhat obscure, with claims having been made by a long list of English, French, German and Swiss inventors. Joshua Shaw[10], an English born American Immigrant, is generally given credit for having developed the first percussion cap in 1814. Shaw patented the percussion cap in America in 1822. The percussion cap was widely used by the 1830s and eventually displaced flintlock ignition by the 1850s[11]. By the late 1860s, center-fire cartridges made the percussion cap system obsolete.

Percussion Revolver Lead Bullets

One unfired .36 caliber, three fired .44 caliber and one unfired conical lead percussion revolver bullets were found (Figure 3.8, Table 3.8). The term percussion revolver[12] refers to the fact that percussion caps were the ignition source for this type of revolver (Illustrations 3.8 and 3.8.1). The percussion revolver was invented by Samuel Colt (1814-1862), of Hartford, Connecticut in the early 1830s. He patented his invention in England in

Figure 3.8 Percussion Revolver Lead Bullets

1835 and in the United States in 1836. When his patent expired in 1857, arms manufacturers in the United States and Europe began to produce percussion revolvers in numerous styles and calibers, with .36 and .44 the most predominant. After the American Civil War, center-fire cartridge revolvers began replacing percussion revolvers.

Rimfire Cartridge Cases

Eleven rimfire cartridge cases, two of which lacked headstamps, were excavated at the Powell site (Tables 3.9 and 3.9.1). A rimfire cartridge "has its primer sealed in and around the rim of its case. The firing pin of a gun striking any part of the rim will ignite the powder charge" (Nonte 1973:215). In 1845, Nicholas Flobert, a Swiss gunsmith living in France, developed a breech loading indoor target rifle that shot a cartridge of his own design called the bulleted breech cap or simply the BB Cap. The cartridge was the size of a percussion cap with a hollow rim containing a percussion sensitive priming compound. A spherical lead bullet of approximately .22 caliber was placed in the mouth of the cartridge and lightly crimped to hold it in place. The priming compound alone provided enough power to propel the bullet at sufficient velocity for short range shooting.

In 1857, Daniel Wesson designed a cartridge based on Flobert's BB Cap. Wesson's design called for a conical shaped bullet in a lengthened case that held a charge of black powder. The new cartridge was called the No. 1 or, 22/100s pistol cartridge, and is known today as the .22 rimfire short. During and after the Civil War, approximately 75 different rimfire cartridge calibers had been developed in America and Europe.

The demise of the rimfire cartridge began around 1900 due to the increasing popularity of the powerful and reloadable center-fire cartridge. By 1918 the number of rimfire cartridge calibers manufactured had declined to 32 types and by the 1930s only 17 different types were manufactured. After World War II, fewer than 10 types of rimfire cartridge calibers were being produced. In the 1950s only the .22 caliber rimfires[13] were still in production.

Center-fire Cartridge Cases

Seven brass center-fire cartridge cases were excavated at the site (Table 3.10). A center-fire cartridge is a cartridge whose primer is located in the center of the base of the case. This is distinguished from a rimfire cartridge which has its primer in the rim (Nonte 1973: 57). The primer in a center-fire cartridge is a cup containing a sensitive explosive compound which, when struck by the firing pin, ignites the powder charge. (Nonte 1973: 195). The center-fire cartridge evolved in the 1860s with the invention of the Berdan and Boxer primers. The Berdan primer, patented on March 20, 1866, is named after its American inventor, Hiram Berdan. The Berdan primer's anvil is formed integrally from the case in the bottom of the primer pocket. The Boxer primer was invented by Edward Boxer of the Royal Arsenal, Woolwich, England and patented on October 13, 1866, and in the U.S. on June 29, 1869. The Boxer primer contains its own anvil pressed into the cup. The two primer systems are not interchangeable, and only Boxer primed cartridges are reloadable. In England and throughout most of the world, center-fire cartridges use Berdan primers. In the United States, Boxer primers are used[14]. The first U.S. center-fire Boxer primed cartridge was the .44 caliber Smith & Wesson American. It was developed in 1866 for the Smith & Wesson, New Model #3 revolver. Today, approximately 100 different calibers of Boxer primed center-fire rifle cartridges and half as many center-fire pistol cartridges are sold in the U.S.

Lead Cartridge Bullets

One cylindro-conical and two cylindro-ogival lead bullets were excavated at the site (Table 3.11). Two of the bullets originated in .22 caliber Long Rifle cartridges. One bullet, possibly .44 caliber, is from a rimfire or center-fire cartridge.

Shotshell

The primerless brass cup is all that remains of a 12 gauge[15] shotshell excavated at the site (Table 3.12). A paper tube once attached to this cup has disintegrated. A shotshell (the technical term for a shotgun shell) is a center fire cartridge that is loaded with either shot, buckshot or a single lead bullet called a slug. Shotshells are used in breech loading shotguns[16]. The first shotshells had a brass case similar to a center-fire cartridge. The Union Metallic Cartridge Company of Bridgeport, Connecticut, began to sell unloaded brass shotshells in 1868, which are said to be the first commercially available shotshells in the USA (Standler 2006). The C.D. Leet Company of Springfield, Massachusetts, began making paper tube shotshells in 1869. With the introduction of plastic tube shotshells in 1960, by the Remington Arms Company, the era of the paper tube shotshell came to an end.

Gun Parts

Eight gun parts were excavated at the site (Table 3.13). All of the gun parts are from muzzle-

loading firearms and probably date to the time of the Powell occupation (see Figure 3.13.2 for an example of such a firearm). The recovered gun parts are: a patchbox lid and a patchbox lid hinge (Figure 3.13.1), three trigger guards (Figure 3.13.3-3.13.7), a gun flint pad (Figure 3.13.8), a flintlock (Figure 3.13.9) and a butt plate (Figures 3.13.11 and 3.13.12 and Illustration 3.13). The unidentified butt plate has the number 215 stamped on the inside.

Figure 3.13.1 Patchbox Lid and Patchbox Lid Hinge

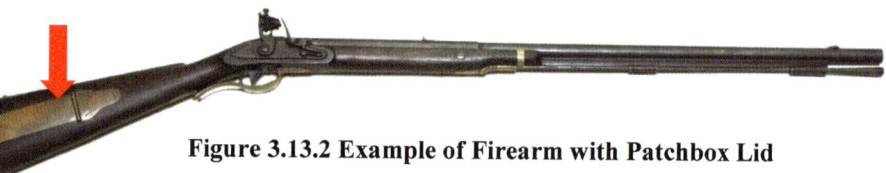

Figure 3.13.2 Example of Firearm with Patchbox Lid

Powder Charge Measure

A powder charge measure was recovered during excavations. Unfortunately, shortly after processing in the lab, this artifact disappeared. Analysis is based on a photograph taken by Houston Archeological Society member Dick Gregg (Figure 3.14, Table 3.14). A powder measure was a volumetric measure which gave a predetermined, uniform charge of black powder. The pioneer rule for ascertaining the correct charge of powder for a round ball rifle was: place a ball

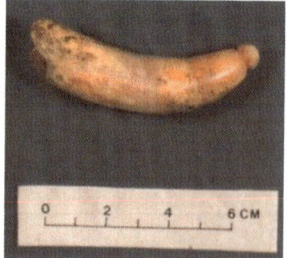

Figure 3.14 Powder Charge Measure

in the palm of the hand and pour out from the powder horn enough powder to completely cover the ball. Then, from a piece of hollowed-out bone or the tip of a small horn, or from a brass tube with a cork in the end, make a charger which this quantity of powder fills exactly to the top (Russell 1957: 231). A measure was usually filled from a powder

Figure 3.13.3 Trigger Guard -- Top View

Figure 3.13.4 Trigger Guard -- Side View

Figure 3.13.5 Brown Bess -- Trigger Guard

Figure 3.13.6 Brown Bess Trigger Guard (showing British "Broad Arrow" emblem)

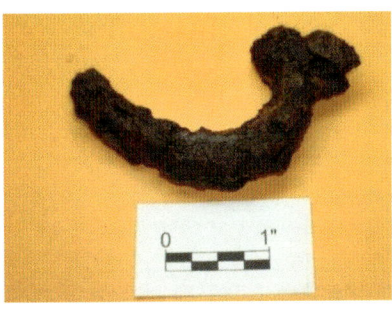

Figure 3.13.7 Trigger Guard

Figure 3.13.8 Gun Flint Pad

Figure 3.13.9 Flintlock

Figure 3.13.11 Unidentified Butt Plate

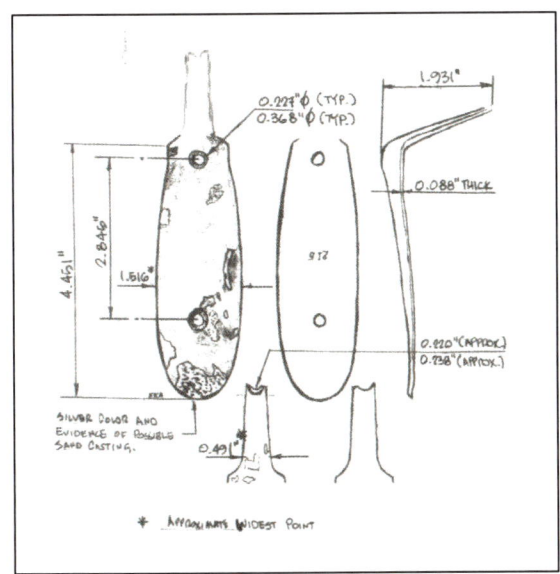

Illustration 3.13 Dimensions of Unidentified Butt Plate

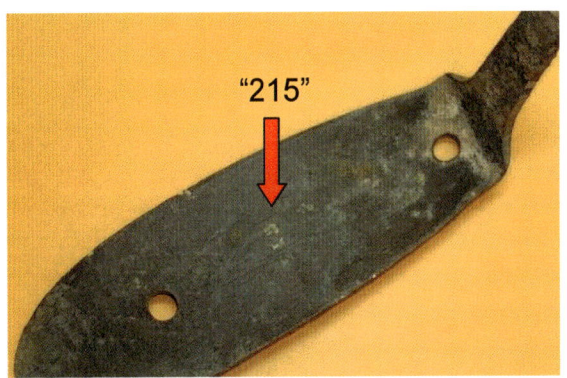

Figure 3.13.12 Inside View of Butt Plate

horn or powder flask containing black powder. From the measure, the black powder was poured down the barrel of a muzzle-loading firearm. Initially, it was assumed by everyone who saw the artifact, including the author, that this measure was made from the tooth of an alligator. However, the measure might have been made from either the 4th protruding tooth of the mandible or one of the protruding teeth in the maxilla (forward of the 4th protruding teeth) near the snout of an American crocodile (Conant 1975: Plate 3, Olsen 1968: 53). The two pair of teeth just described have a slight curve and a "canine" appearance similar to the powder charge measure. All the teeth in an American alligator skull examined by the author have a stubby cylindro-conical shape. It should be noted however, that the skull examined by the author was that of a juvenile that measured 8" long by 4" wide at the base of the skull, perhaps not the best size for making a comparison. The range of the American crocodile occurs from the tip of Florida, including the Florida Keys, and Cuba while the American alligator inhabits Texas, Arkansas, Louisiana, Mississippi, Alabama, Georgia, South Carolina, North Carolina and Florida.

Summary

Of primary interest to the reader is which of these munitions artifacts date to the time of the Elizabeth Powell occupation, circa 1828 to 1836. Let us begin by stating which munitions artifacts post-date the Powell occupation: the percussion revolver bullets, the rimfire cartridge cases, the center-fire cartridge cases, the lead cartridge bullets and the shotshell. The artifacts that probably date to the Powell occupation are the spherical muzzle-loading lead bullets, the unidentified spherical muzzle-loading lead bullet, the lead sprues, the gun flints, the shot and buckshot, the gun parts, and the powder charge measure.

It cannot be accurately determined whether the shot and some of the buckshot date to the Powell occupation due to the fact that it is difficult to differentiate between tower-made shot and buckshot manufactured during the Texas Colonial Period, and more recent tower-made or machine made shot and buckshot. The mold-cast buckshot most likely dates to the Powell occupation.

Percussion caps present another problem. Some believe that weapons using the percussion cap system were in Texas during the Colonial Period. This author has found no evidence to suggest that these types of weapons were in Colonial era Texas[17]. All the artifacts that probably date to the Powell occupation came from or were used in muzzle-loading firearms. Muzzle-loading firearms were used until the end of the Civil War, and these types of artifacts could have been deposited on the site until that time.

Notes:

[1] The location of these units containing munitions artifacts is unknown, and these units are not depicted on the map: M1, M3, M4 and M5.

[2] Beginning with the Model 1795 musket, regulation U.S. muskets had barrel bores of 0.69". Because of crude manufacturing techniques of the period, the diameter was not precise, and good barrels generally ranged from 0.690" to 0.705" diameter. U.S. Military pistols were similarly bored. The use of this system was due in part to the inability of early gunmakers to perform accurate measurements. Precise standard bore diameters did not begin until about 1840, when Sir Joseph Whitworth introduced precise tool making and gauging techniques (NRA 1988: 182). Up through the U.S.-Mexican War, the standard American musket ball had a diameter of 0.640". Early 19th century U.S. Military rifles and rifled pistols had a bore diameter of 0.54". Most of the Mexican army troops that entered San Felipe de Austin in April, 1836, during the Texas War for Independence, were armed with the British India Pattern musket, commonly known by its nick name "Brown Bess." It had a bore diameter of 0.75" and used a lead ball of 0.688" (Hecker & Mauck 1997: 135).

[3] On display in the Alamo Chapel Museum is a Kentucky rifle made by Jacob Dickert (1740-1822) of Lancaster, Pennsylvania. The rifle was supposedly found under some debris by a Mexican peon while completing his military imposed task of carrying the slain Texans to the funeral pyre after the Battle of the Alamo (Hansen 2003: 633).

[4] Ø = Diameter.

[5] For an explanation of the weapons used by the Mexican and Texas Armies during the Texas Revolution, see Borgens, Analysis of the Pass Cavallo Shipwreck, http://handle.tamu.edu/1969.1/586.

[6] To increase the chances of hitting a target with the highly inaccurate smoothbore musket, a paper cartridge called the "buck & ball" was often used. The "buck & ball" cartridge consisted of one musket ball surmounted by three 0.310"Ø buckshot (Thomas 1993: 16).

[7] An economic decision by the United States to restrict American ships and trade to American ports thus eliminating Great Britian's higher quality product.

[8] The Sparks shot tower was the first tower built in the United States in 1808. During the War of 1812 and the Civil War, the Sparks tower produced tons of shot, buckshot and musket balls. It operated until 1903.

[9] Unless cited otherwise, most of the information for this section was from Richard Hamilton's article, *History of the American Shot Tower*, http://www.minnesotatrap.com/history-in-the-making/shot-towers-page-1.htm, accessed August 24, 2014.

[10] See "Joshua Shaw, Artist and Inventor" (*Scientific American* 1869:97) at http://cc.msnscache.com/cache.aspx?q=8340226762003&lang=en-US&mkt=en-US&FORM=CRVE.

[11] The Model 1833 Hall-North U.S. Breech Loading Percussion Carbine, circa 1834-39, was the first weapon adopted officially by the U.S. to use the percussion cap system (Flayderman 1998: 451). The percussion cap system was adapted by the British Army in 1838 (Thomas 2003: 408), the French in 1840 and Austrian Infantry in 1841 (Logan 1959: 4).

[12] Cap and ball revolver was a term commonly applied to these guns. Conical bullets were also fired in these revolvers because of their superior ballistics and penetration power. The purchase of a percussion revolver usually included a bullet mold that cast two bullets, one spherical and one conical.

[13] These were the .22 Short, .22 Long, .22 Long Rifle, .22 Winchester Rimfire (now obsolete), and the .22 Winchester Automatic (now obsolete). In 1959, the .22 WMR or Winchester Magnum Rimfire was introduced. Remington developed the 5mm Rimfire Magnum in 1970. It was discontinued after a few years due to unpopularity. Hornady Manufacturing Company introduced a new rimfire cartridge called the .17 Hornady Magnum in 2002. In 2004, in a joint venture with Cascade Cartridge Co., Hornady developed the .17 caliber Mach II rimfire cartridge.

[14] See http://cc.msnscache.com/cache.aspx?q=8345549347177&lang=en-US&mkt=en-US&FORM=CVRE6.

[15] Gauge sizes in shotguns had a very interesting yet simple origin. In the dim past, someone conceived the idea of designating the size of a shotgun bore from the number of spherical lead balls of that same diameter which could be cast from a pound of lead. The diameter of a lead ball weighing one pound was called a one gauge. That same ball divided equally into four balls of the same diameter gave the size for the four gauge. That pound ball broken down into twelve balls of equal weight and diameter gave us our popular twelve gauge size – and so on for the various gauges. One exception to this common designation of gauges is the present day favorite small .410 shotgun. Its bore diameter is given in thousands of an inch and this designation has applied to both gun and cartridge. (Logan 1959: 172)

[16] Breech loading shotguns began appearing shortly after the American Civil War, replacing muzzle-loading shotguns. Before the 1870s nearly all breech loading shotguns were produced by European gunsmiths. In 1867, Parker Brothers

and Company of West Meridian, Connecticut. used over-stocked Civil War musket parts stored in warehouses to produce shotguns.

[17] Not only a dearth of evidence, but the opinion of the author, rules out the presence of percussion weapons in the Texas Colonial Period. The author likes this quote from Worman (2007:44): "In the wilderness of the American west, some at first were reluctant to abandon the time-tested flintlock, for if a hunter or trapper was far from a source of percussion caps, his gun was useless when his supply was exhausted. However, it was often possible to locate and shape a piece of flint to fit between the jaws of a flint-lock hammer." The reader should be aware that some of the firearms supposedly used by members of the Texas Army in the Texas Revolution and displayed in museums, were originally flint-locks that were eventually converted to the percussion cap system. A good example of this are the two Kentucky pistols supposedly owned by Stephen F. Austin and pictured in Cantrell (1999: 91). These two pistols were originally flintlocks that were converted to the percussion cap system. It can be clearly seen in the picture that the flashpans have been replaced by bolsters on these two pistols.

References and Other Resources

Ahern, Bill
   2005   *Muskets of the Revolution and the French & Indian Wars.* Andrew Mowbray Publishers, Lincoln, RI

Aucoin, Elizabeth K., Pablo R. Castro, Sheldon M. Kindall and Robert T. Shelby
   2002   *The Elizabeth Powell Site (41FB269) Fort Bend County, Texas.* Houston Archeological Society Report No. 25, Part 1. Edited by Elizabeth K. Aucoin and Linda L. Swift. Houston Archeological Society, Houston, TX

Baker, Lindsay T. and Billy R. Harrison
   1986   *Adobe Walls: The History and Archeology of the 1874 Trading Post.* Texas A&M Univ. Press, College Station, TX

Barber, John L.
   1987   *The Rimfire Cartridge in the United States & Canada: 1857-1984.* Armory Publications, Tacoma, WA

Barnes, Frank C.
   2006   *Cartridges of the World.* 11th Edition. Gun Digest Books, Iola, WI

Borgens, Amy A.
   2004   *Analysis of the Pass Cavallo Shipwreck.* Unpublished Masters Thesis, Texas A&M University. Electronic document, http://handle.tamu.edu/1969.1/586 (accessed 9-2009)

Cantrell, Gregg
   1999   *Stephen F. Austin: Empresario of Texas.* Yale University Press, New Haven, CT, & London, England

Carter, Samuel
   1971   *Blaze of Glory: The Fight for New Orleans, 1814-1815.* St. Martin's Press, New York, NY

Coates, Earl J. and Dean S. Thomas
   1990   *An Introduction to Small Arms Ammunition.* Thomas Publications, Gettysburg, PA

Conant, Isabelle H.
   1975   *A Field Guide to Reptiles and Amphibians of Eastern and Central North America.* Houghton Mifflin Company, Boston MA

Darling, Anthony D.
   1970   *Red Coat and Brown Bess: Historical Arms Series No. 12.* Museum Restoration Services, Alexandria Bay, NY. Bloomfield, Ontario, Canada

Dillin, John G.W.
   1967   *The Kentucky Rifle.* 5th ed. George Shumway, York, PA

Dimmick, Gregg J.
   2004   *Sea of Mud: The Retreat of the Mexican Army after San Jacinto: An Archeological Investigation.* Texas State Historical Association, Austin, TX

Dixie Gun Works
   2008   *Catalog #157.* Union City, TN

Flayderman, Norm
   1998   *Flayderman's Guide to Antique American Firearms and Their Values.* Krause Publications, Iola, WI

Hamilton, Richard
   2013   *History of the American Shot Tower.* http://minnesotatrap.com/history-in-the-making/shot-towers-page-1.htm (accessed 8-24-2014)

Hamilton, T.M., Editor
   1982   *Indian Trade Guns.* Pioneer Press, Union City, TN

HAS Report No. 25, Part 3   Page 41

Haecker, Charles M. and Jeffrey G. Mauck
    1997   *On the Prairie of Palo Alto: Historical Archaeology of the U.S.-Mexican War Battlefield.* Texas A&M University Press, College Station, TX

Hansen, Todd, Editor
    2003   *The Alamo Reader: A Study in History.* Stackpole Books, Mechanicsburg, PA

Hanson, Charles E. Jr.
    1992   *The Northwest Gun.* The Museum Association of the American Frontier, Chadron, NE

Hatch, Alden
    1956   *Remington Arms: An American History.* Rinehart & Co., Inc., New York, NY and Toronto, Canada

Hogg, Ian V,
    1982   *The Cartridge Guide: The Small Arms Ammunition Identification Manual.* Stackpole Books, Harrisburg, PA

Hudgins, Joe D.
    1984   *Post West Bernard 1837-1839. 41WH16.* Houston Archeological Society Journal No. 80

Hudgins, Joe D., Terry Kieler and Gregg Dimmick
    1999   *Tracking the Mexican Army through the Mar de Lodo (Sea of Mud), April 29-May 9, 1836.* 41WH93, 41WH94,41WH95. Houston Archeological Society Report No. 16
    2009   Personal communication

Kelly, Jack
    2004   *Gunpowder: Alchemy, Bombards, & Pyrotechnics: The History of the Explosive that Changed the World.* Basic Books, New York, NY

Labadie, Joseph H., Kenneth M. Brown, Anne A. Fox, Samuel P. Nesmith, Paul S. Storch, David D. Turner, Shirley Van der Veer and Alisa J. Winkler
    1986   *La Villita Earthworks: A Preliminary Report of Investigations of Mexican Siege Works at the Battle of the Alamo (41BX677): San Antonio, Texas.* Center for Archaeological Research, The University of Texas at San Antonio, Archaeological Survey Report No. 153

Logan, Herschel C.
    1959   *Cartridges: A Pictorial Digest of Small Arms Ammunition.* Bonanza Books, New York, NY

Marcott, Roy
    2005   *The History of Remington Firearms.* The Lyons Press, Guilfort, CT

Mason, M.E. Jr. and W. Reid McKee
    1980   *Civil War Projectiles II: Small Arms and Field Artillery.* Rapidan Press, Mechanicsville, VA

Minchinton, Walter
    1990   *The Shot Tower.* http://americanheritage.com/articles/magazine/it/1990/1/1990_1_52.shtml (accessed 8-27-2007)

Neuman, George C.
    1998   *Battle Weapons of the American Revolution.* Scurlock Publishing Co., Inc., Texarkana, TX

Nonte, George C. Jr.
    1973   *Firearms Encyclopedia.* Harper and Row, New York, NY

NRA (National Rifle Association)
    1988   *NRA Firearms Fact Book.* Publication of the National Rifle Association, Washington D.C.

Olson, Stanley J.
    1968   *Fish, Amphibian and Reptile Remains From Archaeological Sites, Part 1: Southeastern and Southwestern United States.* Peabody Museum, Cambridge, MA

Rains, Richard L.
    2006   *Winchester, Two-piece .22 Boxes, 1873 to 1927.* Rowe Publications, Rochester, NY

Remington Arms Co. and The Union Metallic Cartridge Co.
1962   *1910 Illustrated Catalog.* New York: M. Hartley Co., 1910. Reproduced by permission of Remington Arms Co., California: Jayco, 1962

Russell, Carl P.
1957   *Guns on the Early Frontiers: A History of Firearms from Colonial Times through the Years of the Western Fur Trade.* University of Nebraska Press, Lincoln, NE and London, UK

Scientific American
1869   *Joshua Shaw, Artist and Inventor*, Vol. 21, No. 7, New York, NY (accessed 8-14-2014)

Scott, Douglas D., Richard A. Fox, Melissa A. Connor and Dick Harmon
1989   *Archaeological Perspectives on the Battle of the Little Bighorn.* University of Oklahoma Press, Norman, OK, and London, UK

Serven, James E.
1981   *Colt Firearms from 1836.* 3rd Edition. Stackpole Books, Harrisburg, PA

Shuey, Daniel L.
1999   *W.R.A. Co.: Headstamped Cartridges and Their Variations, Volume I.* WCF Publications, Inc., Rockford, IL
2003   *W.R.A. Co.: Headstamped Cartridges and Their Variations, Volume II.* WCF Publications, Inc., Rockford, IL

Stadt, Ronald W.
1984   *Winchester Shotguns and Shotshells.* Armory Publications, Tacoma, WA

Standler, Ronald B.
2006   *Shotshell Cartridge History.* http://www.rhs0.com/shotshell.htm (accessed 5-3-2007)

Suydam, Charles R.
1960   *The American Cartridge.* G. Robert Lawrence, Publisher, Santa Ana, CA
1979   *U.S. Cartridges and Their Handguns: 1795-1975.* Beinfeld Publishing, Inc., North Hollywood, CA

Thomas, Dean S.
1993   *Ready...Aim...Fire!: Small Arms Ammunition in the Battle of Gettysburg.* Thomas Publications, Gettysburg, PA
1997   *Round Ball to Rimfire: A History of Small Arms Ammunition: Part 1.* Thomas Publications, Gettysburg, PA
2002   *Round Ball to Rimfire: A History of Small Arms Ammunition: Part II.* Thomas Publications, Gettysburg, PA
2003   *Round Ball to Rimfire: A History of Small Arms Ammunition: Part III.* Thomas Publications, Gettysburg, PA.

Thomas, James E. and Dean S. Thomas
1996   *A Handbook of Civil War Bullets & Cartridges.* Thomas Publications, Gettysburg, PA

Walter, John
1998   *The Guns That Won the West: Firearms on the American Frontier, 1848-1898.* Greenhill Books, London, Stackpole Books, Mechanicsburg, PA

Worman, Charles C.
2007   *Firearms in American History.* Westholme Publications, LLC, Yardley, PA

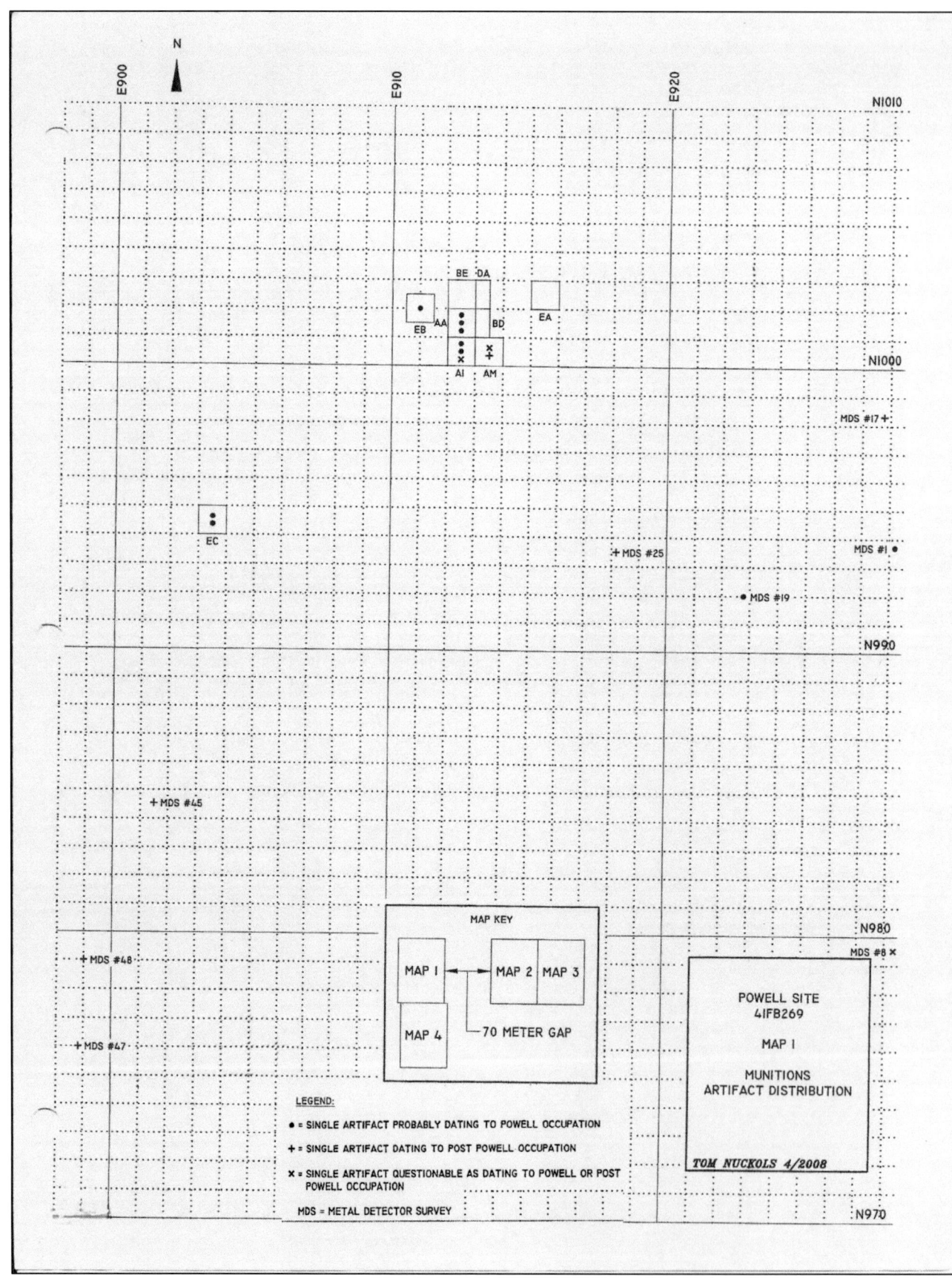

Map 3.1 West Section of Site

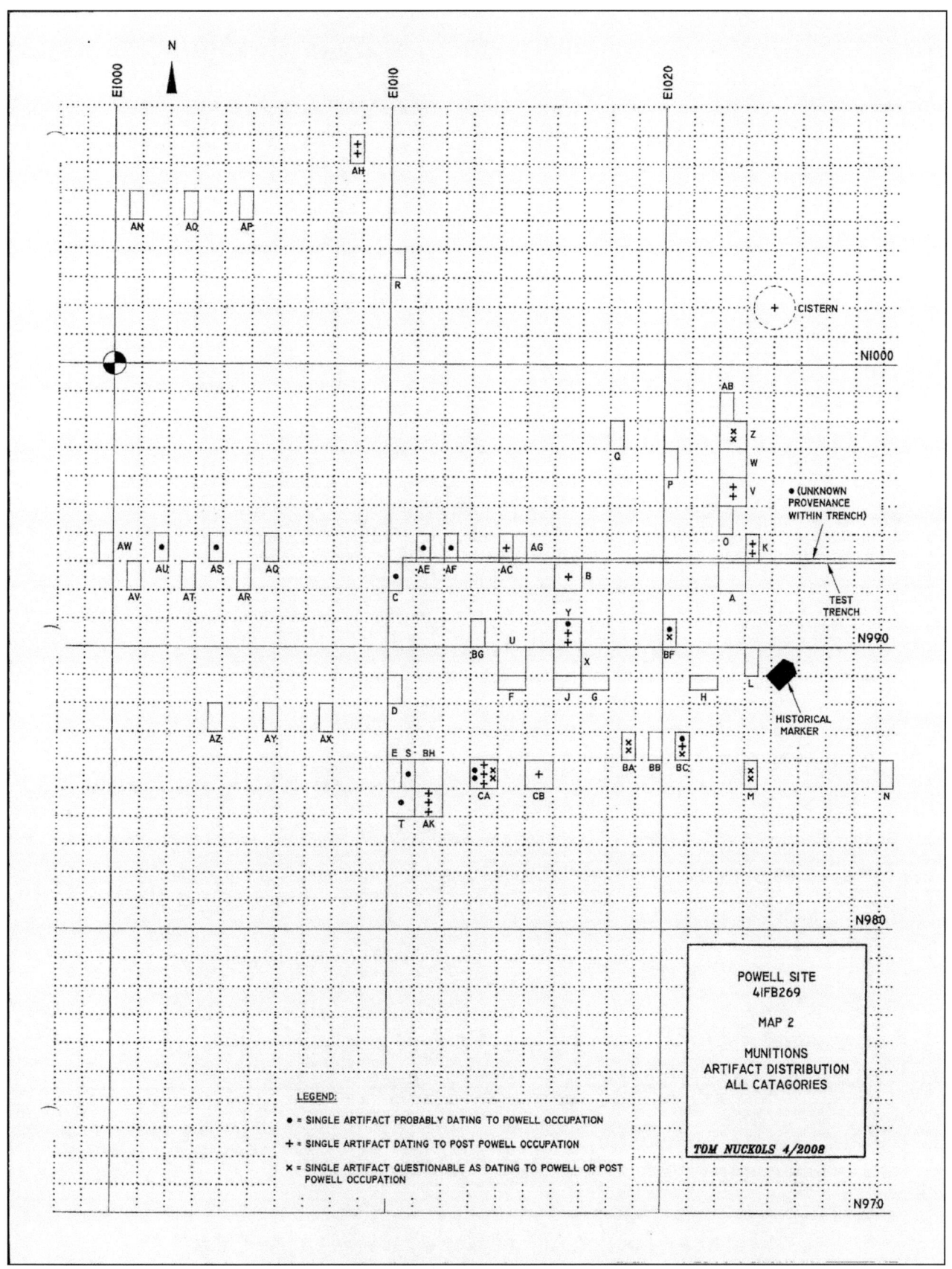

Map 3.2 Main Map Showing Datum and Historical Marker

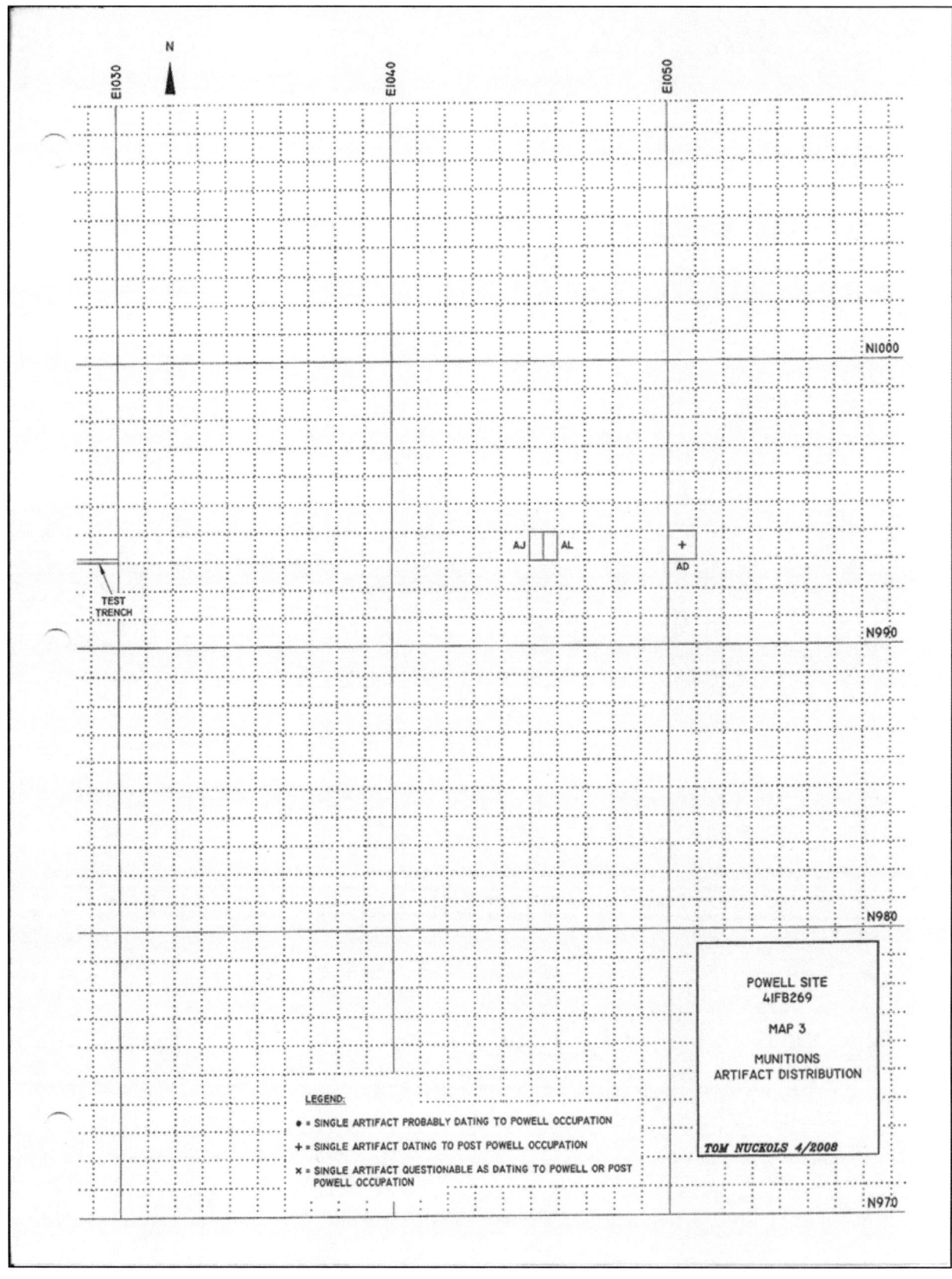

Map 3.3 Section Adjacent to East Side of Main Map

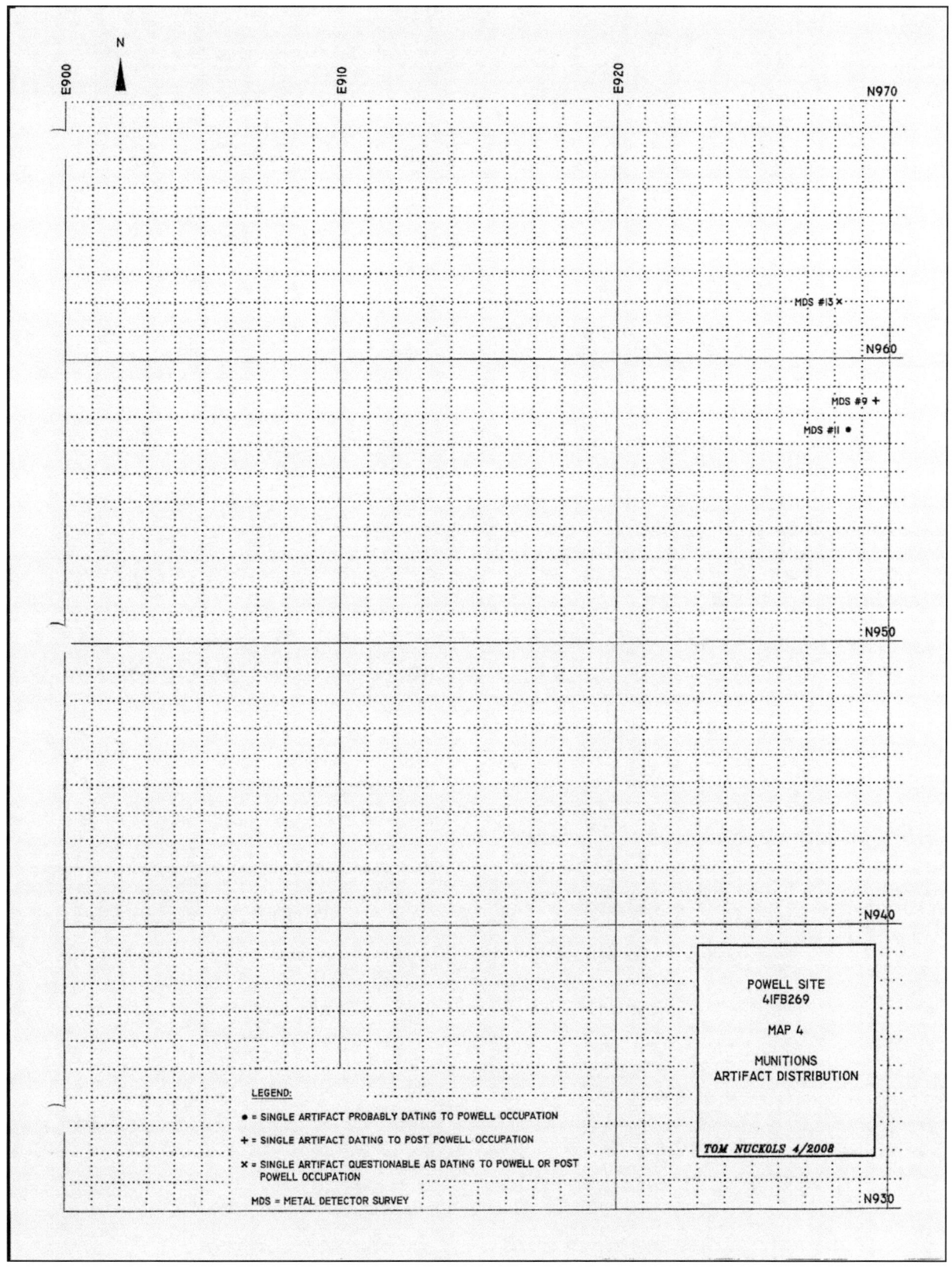

Map 3.4 Section South of West Section (Map 3.1)

Table 3.1: Spherical Muzzle-loading Lead Bullets

Catalog #	Unit	Level	Depth cm	Grain Weight	Approximate Diameter	Comments
338	AE	3	10-15	134.7	?	Fired. One side flattened by impact. No visible sprue nib or mold seam. Impact diameter approximately 0.50". Original diameter indeterminable.
1067-1	AI	3	10-15	137.7	0.479"	Unfired. Slightly out of round. Partial mold seam present.
2132-1	M5	2	5-10	149.6	?	Fired. One side flattened by impact. No sprue nib visible. Mold seam present on undamaged side. Impact diameter approximately 0.545". Original diameter indeterminable.
2157	M3	5	20-25	152.7	0.484"	Unfired. Slightly out of round. Sprue nib and partial mold seam present.
2842	MDS #1	-	-	86.8	0.435"	Fired. One side flattened by impact. Very pronounced sprue nib and mold seam present.
2848	MDS #11	-	-	95.9	?	Fired. One side flattened by impact. No sprue nib or mold seam visible. Impact diameter approximately 0.50". Original diameter indeterminable.

Table 3.2: Unidentified Spherical Muzzle-loading Lead Bullet

Catalog #	Unit	Level	Depth cm	Grain Weight	Approximate Diameter	Comments
512-1	BC	3	10-15	265.5	0.608"	Unfired. Probably cast in a worn mold, giving it a slightly elliptical shape of 0.608"Ø X 0.616" long. Sprue still attached and very pronounced mold seam present. Sprue is 0.314"Ø X 0.369" long. At the bottom of the bullet, the mold seam extends approximately 0.10" above the surface.

Table 3.3: Lead Sprues

Catalog #	Unit	Level	Depth cm	Grain Weight	Approximate Stem Dimensions	Comments
749-2	Y	5	20-25	21.3	0.250" Ø X 0.185" long.	-
1263-2	M1	5	20-25	31.2	Rectangular shaped, 0.190" X 0.245". The stem does not protrude far enough past the cap to obtain a length measurement.	-
2243	M4	2	5-10	40.6	0.137"Ø X 0.154" long.	These two sprues are combined because the stems appear the same (somewhat cone shaped), and their measurements are almost identical. This suggests that they were cut off bullets that were cast in the same mold.
2728	CA	3	10-15	27.1	0.132"Ø X 0.159" long.	

Table 3.4: Gun Flints

Catalog #	Unit	Level	Depth cm	Comments
336	AF	2	5-10	This is a musket flint. Due to extensive wear, it is impossible to determine its striking edge.
1181	AA	4	15-20	This is a musket flint that is broken off at the back. It is honey colored indicating a possible French origin.
1496	T	12	60-65	This is possibly a rifle, pistol or shotgun flint.
2521	AS	4	15-20	The striking edge of this flint is broken off.
2705	EC	5	20-25	This is a musket flint. It is honey colored indicating a possible French origin.
2813	EB	2	5-10	This is possibly a rifle, pistol or shotgun flint.
2829	EC	5	20-25	This is possibly a rifle, pistol or shotgun flint.

Table 3.5: Lead Shot

Catalog #	Unit	Level	Depth cm	Approximate diameter	Weight in grains	Comments
1084-1	AM	3	10-15	0.146"	4.2	Oxidized.

Table 3.6: Lead Buckshot

Catalog #	Unit	Level	Depth	Approximate diameter	Weight in grains	Comments[1]
191	BA	2	5-10	0.255"	28.9	-
197	BA	3	10-15	0.286"	29.5	-
563	M	1	0-5	0.249"	22.6	-
685	M	3	10-15	0.285"	31.2	-
1067-2	AI	3	10-15	0.281"	33.2	-
1136-1	Z	3	10-15	0.325"	41.8	-
1136-2	Z	3	10-15	0.336"	28.9	An insufficient amount of molten lead was poured in the mold when this buckshot was cast resulting in half a sphere. Distinct mold seam present on spherical side.
1625	BF	1	0-5	0.253"	27.4	Sprue nib present; no mold seam visible.
1633-2	BF	2	5-10	0.255"	24.6	Distinct mold seam present; no sprue nib visible.
1732	BC	2	5-10	0.334"	58.3	Sprue nib and partial mold seam present.
2037	CA	5	20-25	0.316"	45.2	-
2051	CA	4	15-20	0.278"	33.1	-
2846	MDS #8	-	-	0.327"		-

[1] All of the buckshot exhibit some degree of oxidization. No attempt has been made to document all of the surface irregularities (dimples, cuts, facets), present on these buckshot; they are too numerous. No distinction has been made indicating whether the buckshot is unfired or fired. Because of their small size and light weight buckshot can impact and incur damage that is indistinguishable from damage derived from several other ways, such as compression in a shotshell or battering in a shot pouch carried by users of muzzle-loading shotguns.

Table 3.7: Percussion Caps

Catalog #	Unit	Level	Depth	Material	Approximate Dimensions	Comments	Firearm Signatures
1084-2	AM	3	10-15	Copper	0.183"Ø X 0.133" long	Plain wall; Unknown size [1].	Partial rammer imprint present on flattened side. Only one rifling groove visible, approximately 0.072" wide, twist direction indeterminable[2].
1923	CB	5	20-25	Copper	0.220"Ø X 0.259" long	Ribbed wall; Unknown size.	None; probably obliterated by impact.

Table 3.8: Percussion Revolver Lead Bullets

Catalog #	Unit	Level	Depth	Weight in Grains	Caliber & Type	Description	Firearm Signatures
261	BC	1	0-5 cm	110.0	.44 Spherical	Fired. One side flattened by impact. No sprue nib or mold seam visible. Impact diameter is approximately 0.478"	
706	K	3	10-15 cm	81.7	.44 Spherical	Fired. One side flattened by impact with a "crinkled" appearance suggesting impact with the earth. No sprue or mold seam visible. Impact diameter is approximately 0.463"	

[1] As far as the author can determine, percussion caps manufactured in the U.S. came in these sizes: Colt's Pistol, 9, 10, 11, 12, 13, 14, 18 and Musket. Other than the musket cap, diligent research by the author has failed to reveal the dimensions for the sizes of these percussion caps. A tin container of percussion caps examined by the author is a good example of the frustration of trying to equate dimensions to cap sizes. The printing on the lid of the container says: FOIL LINED PERCUSSION CAPS. UNION METALLIC CARTRIDGE CO. BRIDGEPORT,C.T. No size is listed. Inside the container are 50 ribbed caps, each with a dimension of 0.208"Ø X 0.209" long. An Eley Brothers (London manufacturer of guns and ammunition) advertising sheet, circa 1865, lists these sizes of percussion caps for sale: 5 (43), 6 (44), 7 (46), 8 (48), 9 (49), 24 (50), 10 (51 & 52), 11 (53 & 54), 18 (55 & 56), 12 (57), 13 (58) and 14. The numbers in parenthesis are caps that correspond with Birmingham sizes (Thomas 2003: 428). In 1956, excavations conducted at the site of Fort Pierre II, a post of the American Fur Company, circa 1859-1863, uncovered 14 ribbed, copper percussion caps. The dimensions given for these caps are 0.011" thick, 0.266" long and 0.175"Ø. They are said to be #12 or #13 rifle or pistol caps and due to their thick walls are probably of English manufacture (Caldwell in Hamilton 1982: 121). Excavations conducted in 1975 at the Adobe Walls site (unknown trinomial), an 1874 trading post in the Texas Panhandle, yielded 26 percussion caps. 23 of these caps were measurable. Based on the 1st Edition of Frank C. Barnes, *Cartridges of the World*, published in 2006, the authors were able to identify 5 different cap sizes. One cap is 0.17"Ø X 0.17" long and identified as an RSW Sinoxid #1075. One cap is 0.18"Ø X 0.24" long and identified as a Remington #13. Two caps are 0.242"Ø X 0.24" long and identified as #EB. Five caps are 0.183" Ø X 0.21" long and identified as #21. Fourteen caps are 0.18"Ø X 0.21" long and identified as Eley-Kynoch #18 or Remington #12 (Baker & Harrison 1986: 197-198).

Musket caps were about the size of a pencil eraser and were referred to as "top hat caps" because they resembled a tiny top hats. They had a body diameter of 0.206", a split flange or "brim" diameter of 0.300" and a length of 0.217".

[2] Depending on the firearms manufacturer, rifling either twists to the right or left. This applies to both antique and modern firearms.

Table 3.8 (continued)

777	Y	4	15-20 cm	83.1	.44 Spherical	Fired. One side flattened by impact. No sprue nib visible. Partial mold seam present on undamaged side. Impact diameter is approximately 0.459".	Three possible rifling imprints, but hard to distinguish due to impact damage.
1263-1	MI	5	20-25 cm	84.0	.36 Spherical	Unfired. Sprue nib and mold seam present. Diameter is approximately 0.377".	-
2851	MDS #25	-	-	178.1	.44 Conical	Unfired. Rebated base[3]; pointed nose. 0.445" diameter X 0.653" long (including rebated base). Rebated base diameter is 0.395" X 0.75" long. No sprue nib visible, but mold seam present.	-

---

[3] Serven (1981: 83) calls the rebated base a "perceptible band" and states that its purpose was to start the bullet more easily in the cylinder chamber. Beginning circa 1850 the rebated base was used as an attachment point for a combustible cartridge.

Table 3.9: Rimfire Cartridge Cases

Catalog #	Unit	Level	Depth	Caliber	Case Material	Headstamp	Firing Pin Imprint Shape	Comments
527	K	1	0-5 cm	.22 Short	Oxidized Brass[1]	C[2]	■A	Case has two knurled cannelures.
829	V	3	10-15 cm	.22 Short	Copper	US[3]	●	-
1236	AK	1	0-5 cm	.22 Short	?	None. See Table 3.9.1	■	Due to corrosion, case material is indeterminable.
1251	AK	2	5-10 cm	.22 Short	Brass	H[4]	●B	-
1805	V	1	5-10 cm	.22 Short	Oxidized Brass	C	■A	Case has two knurled cannelures.
1952-1	CA	3	10-15 cm	.22 Short	Nickel Plated Brass[5]	H	■C	Nickel plated case.
1952-2	CA	3	10-15 cm	.22 Short	Nickel Plated Brass	H	■C	Nickel plated case.
2038	CA	5	20-25 cm	.22 Short	Nickel Plated Brass	H	■C	Nickel plated case.
2502	AH	4	15-20 cm	.22 Short	Brass	H	●B	-
1816	Cistern	3	10-15 cm	.22 Long or Long Rifle[6]	Copper Washed Brass[7]	H	■	-
168	B	3	10-15 cm	.38 Short[8]	?	None. See Table 3.9.1	■(2)	Two firing pin imprints, approx. 23° apart, indicate that this cartridge misfired once. Due to corrosion, case material is indeterminable.

Comments:
1. All the cases in this collection are the rimmed straight type.
2. All the headstamps in this collection are the impressed type.
3. Extractor marks were not discernable on any of the cases.
4. Cartridge cases with a rectangular firing pin imprint (squares above) were fired in a pistol or revolver. A circular firing imprint indicates a case fired in a rifle.
5. Firing pin imprints appear identical from firearm to firearm within a single type. Unique variations to each firing pin allow identification of cartridges fired in the same firearm. Matching firing pin imprints are designated by a corresponding letter next to the firing pin imprint shape.

[1] One of the many materials that Cascade Cartridge Inc., used for their .22 rimfire cartridge case was oxidized brass. The reason for this is unknown. Oxidized brass cases have a shiny brown appearance.
[2] C = Cascade Cartridge Incorporated, Lewiston, ID. On September 22, 1955, Cascade Cartridge Inc. was incorporated in Idaho. Lewiston was the plant site. Until early 1963 when the first .22 Long Rifle cartridges were made and sold, the company was a major primer and rim fire industrial tool blank manufacturer. Over the next several years, the .22 Short, Long and Winchester Magnum Rimfire cartridges were added to the product line. In 1967, the company was acquired by Omark Industries, Inc. and operated first as Omark C.C.I., Inc. This was changed to CCI-Operations, Sporting Equipment Division, Omark Industries Inc., and after the purchase of Speer, Inc. in 1975, to CCI-Speer Operations, Sporting Goods Equipment Division, Omark Industries, Inc. The company is still in business (Barber 1987: 89).

3 US = United States Cartridge Company, Lowell, MA. Former Union Army Brigadier General Benjamin F. Butler and a group of associates founded the United States Cartridge Co. (USC) in Lowell, Massachusetts. Incorporation was on June 14, 1869. Rim and center fire cartridge production began in late 1869. Raised and impressed headstamps on rimfire cartridges began circa 1885. On February 7, 1890, two of the company's powder magazines exploded with a loss of twenty-two lives and considerable property damage to the town of Lowell. In 1909, National Lead Co. acquired a 50% interest in USC. Two years after Butler's death in 1918, National bought the remaining interest. Winchester Repeating Arms Co. purchased USC's machinery and equipment from National in 1926. Winchester continued to manufacture United States Cartridge Co. ammunition until 1936 (Barber 1987: 40-42, 51-54, 85).

4 H = Winchester Repeating Arms Company, New Haven, CT. On May 30, 1866, The New Haven Arms Co. became the Winchester Repeating Arms Co. Rimfire metallic cartridges manufactured by Winchester were headstamped with a raised "H" in an impressed circle. The headstamp was created to honor to B. Tyler Henry who, in 1860, invented the Henry lever action rifle with its .44 caliber metallic rimfire cartridge. The Henry was the precursor to the early Winchester Lever Action Rifles. For a brief period in 1880, a raised "W" headstamp was put on .22 and .41 caliber short rimfire cartridges as a tribute to Oliver Fisher Winchester who died on December 10, 1880. Between 1880 and 1895 the original headstamp was phased out on all calibers under and including .41, and was replaced with a small impressed "H" in a small depressed circle, followed by a large impressed "H". In 1895, a small impressed "H" became the standard. On January 31, 1931 Western Cartridge Co. purchased Winchester. Western continues to make Winchester brand .22 caliber rimfire ammunition with the small impressed "H" headstamp (Barber 1987: 11-12, 55-58, 87-88).

5 Suydam (1960: 51) states that the nickeled case identified early "Super Speed" rounds. Winchester began using the "Super Speed" brand name in 1925 (Shuey 1999: 71). "Super X" brand ammunition replaced "Super Speed" circa 1934. The "SUPER X" headstamp replaced the "H" headstamp used on "Super Speed" rimfire cartridges.

6 Both the Long and Long Rifle rimfire cartridge share the same case length of 0.600". The longer, heavier bullet in the latter differentiates the two. Information about the .22 Long cartridge is sketchy. It was listed in the 1871 Great Western Gun Works catalog for the seven shot Standard revolver. A few years later, gun companies began making rifles that used this cartridge. The .22 Long cartridge was first listed in Winchester catalogues in 1873 (Rains 2006: 14). Currently, only Cascade Cartridge Co., and Remington Arms Co., manufacture this cartridge. The .22 Long Rifle cartridge was developed by the J. Stevens Arms & Tool Company in 1887. The Union Metallic Cartridge Co., began selling the .22 Long Rifle cartridge in 1884; Winchester in 1890 (Rains 2006: 110). The .22 Long Rifle cartridge is one of the most popular rimfires in the world and manufactured in every country producing ammunition (Barnes 2006: 477).

7 This case has a dark red color. Shuey (1999: 18) offers a possible explanation: what appears to be "Red Brass" has been observed on a very few early casings. This material is brass, but with a thin layer of copper applied to the case wall. This gives the cartridge more of a reddish hue. This process was quite popular with the United States Cartridge Company in the late 1800s, but not with Winchester. Barber (1987: 169) states that Winchester experimentally tried copper washed brass cases in the early 1880s with no public acceptance. No information has been found that explains the advantages of applying copper to a brass cartridge case.

8 Walter (1999: 251) states that this cartridge was introduced during the American Civil War though details remain elusive. The only two firearms that used this cartridge during the Civil War were the Prescott and Bacon revolvers. By 1875, Allen, Colt and Remington revolvers and Ballard, Remington, Stevens and Frank Wesson rifles were available in .38 Short. It was discontinued in 1939.

Table 3.9.1: Unheadstamped Rimfire Cartridge Cases

Two rimfire cartridge cases in the Powell Site collection are unheadstamped: a .22 caliber Short, Catalog #1263, and a .38 caliber Short, Catalog #168. The manufacturers of these cases are unknown[1]. Below is a list of companies that manufactured or sold unheadstamped rimfires.

Company	Unheadstamped Rimfires Produced	Years in Business
Allen & Wheelock Worcester, MA	.38 Short	1858-1864
Crittenden & Tibbals South Coventry, CT	.22 Short, .38 Short	1862-1864
Crittenden & Tibblas Manufacturing Co. South Coventry, CT	.22 Short, .38 Short	1864-1866
Christian D. Sharps & Co. Philadelphia, PA	.22 Short, .38 Short	1858~1861
Dominion Cartridge Co. Brownsburg, Quebec	.22 Short, .38 Short	1886-1976 Rimfire cartridges headstamped "D" beginning in the 1890s.
Ethan Allen Worcester, MA	.22 Short, .38 Short	1864
Ethan Allen & Co. Worchester, MA	.22 Short, .38 Short	1865-1871
Forehand & Wadsworth Worcester, MA	.22 Short, .38 Short	1871-1874
Hall & Hubbard Springfield, MA	.22 Short, .38 Short	1869-1874
H.C. Lombard & Co. Springfield, MA	.22 Short	1860-1862
H.W. Mason New York, NY	.22 Short	1870
H.W. Mason South Coventry, CT	.22 Short	1870-1877
Leet, Goff & Co. Springfield, MA	.22 Short	1860-1862
National Cartridge Co. Belleville, IL	.22 Short	1908-1909

Table 3.9.1 (continued)

Phoenix Metallic Cartridge Co. South Coventry, CT	.22 Short, .38 Short	1874-1891 Rimfire cartridges headstamped "P" beginning circa 1878.
Sears, Roebuck & Co. Chicago, IL	.22 Short	1908-mid 1930s[2]
Sharps & Hawkins Philadelphia, PA	.22 Short, .38 Short	1862-1867
Smith, Hall & Farmer Springfield, MA	.22 Short, .38 Short	1865-1866
Smith, Hall & Buckland Springfield, MA	.22 Short, .38 Short	1866-1869
Smith & Wesson Springfield, MA	.22 Short	1857-1860
Union Metallic Cartridge & Cap Co. Bridgeport, CT	.22 Short	1866-1867
Union Metallic Cartridge Co. Bridgeport, CT	.22 Short, .38 Short	1867-to date. Rimfire cartridges headstamped "U" beginning 1885.
United States Cartridge Co. Lowell, MA	.22 Short, .38 Short	1869-1926. Rimfire cartridges headstamped "US" beginning circa 1885.

---

[1] One method used to identify an unheadstamped cartridge case is by the presence of tool marks on the rim or base. One of the most critical stages in rimfire cartridge manufacture was the crimp; it had to be tightly closed and so arranged that the axis of the bullet was maintained. That this was a continuing problem in the early years can be demonstrated by the number of changes in the tool points of the power head that turned the case. Each is a hallmark of a particular manufacturer. By 1900 crimping methods that left no marks had been developed by most companies; the one exception, USC, followed suit in 1908 to 1910 (Barber 1987: 185). No tool marks were found on the cases.

[2] In 1908 Western Cartridge Co., acquired a contract to supply Sears with .22 Short rimfire cartridges. At the request of Sears, these cartridges were unheadstamped. Sears sold these .22s under the Meridan and Clinton Cartridge Corp. label until the mid 1930s.

Table 3.10: Center-fire Cartridge Cases

Catalog #	Unit	Level	Depth	Caliber	Case Type	Headstamp	Match	Comments
2855	MDS #45	-	-	.243 Winchester[1]	A	R-P 243 WIN[2]	-	This and the 3 following rifle cases were probably deposited on the site in the recent past by deer hunters.
2857	MDS #48	-	-	7mm Remington Magnum[3]	B	FC 7mm REM MAG[4]	-	-
2850	MDS #17	-	-	.308 Winchester[5]	A	R-P 308 WIN	A	-
2856	MDS #47	-	-	.308 Winchester	A	R-P 308 WIN	A	-
428	AC	3	10-15 cm	.45 Colt[6]	C	None[7]	B	Copper primer approx. 0.145"Ø.
576-1	M	2	5-10 cm	.45 Colt	C	U.M.C. .45 COLT.[8]	-	Copper primer approx. 0.225"Ø. This cartridge was manufactured by the Union Metallic Cartridge Company before circa 1916[9]. The period after the word "COLT" signifies a variant[10].
794-1	Y	5	20-35 cm	.45 Colt	C	None	B	Same as Catalog #428. These two cartridges were probably manufactured by the same company.

Comments:

1. Extractor marks were not discernible on any of the cases.
2. Case types are:
   A - Rimless bottleneck. Solid head with solid web.
   B - Belted bottleneck. Solid head with solid web
   C - Rimmed straight. Solid head with button primer pocket
3. No matter what type of firearm a center-fire cartridge is fired in, the primer will have a circular firing pin imprint. Unique variations to each firing pin allow identification of cartridges fired in the same gun. Matching firing pin imprints are designated by corresponding letters in the "Match" column.

---

[1] The .243 Winchester was introduced by Winchester in 1955 as a rifle cartridge. The .243 is adequate for hunting small game up to and including deer and antelope (Barnes 2006: 26).

[2] R-P = Remington – Peters. In 1884, Winchester and the Union Metallic Cartridge Company jointly purchased Remington, a manufacturer of firearms and ammunition. In 1896, UMC purchased Winchester's share of Remington. In 1933, DuPont acquired 60% of UMC and Remington. In 1980, DuPont purchased the remaining stock in Remington, and Remington then became a wholly-owned subsidiary of DuPont. Peters Cartridge Corporation was founded in 1887 in Cincinnati, Ohio. In 1934, Remington purchased Peters. In 1944, production at Peters the plant in Ohio stopped. After 1944, Peters ammunition was made in Remington's plant, and was identical to the Remington product (Standler 2006).

[3] The 7mm Remington Magnum was introduced by Remington in 1962. It is a long-range big game rifle cartridge. In rifle caliber's, a magnum designation generally refers to a belted case loaded to higher than normal pressure, velocity and energy levels for the particular bullet diameter (Nonte 1973: 157).

[4] FC = Federal Cartridge. Federal Cartridge Corporation was incorporated in Minneapolis, Minnesota in 1922.

[5] The .308 (7.62x51mm NATO) was introduced by Winchester as a sporting rifle cartridge in 1952. It was adapted as the official U.S. Military rifle cartridge in 1954.

[6] One of the most famous American handgun cartridges, the .45 Colt was introduced in 1873 by Colt Firearms for their Single Action Army revolver, a.k.a. "Model 1873", "Model P", "Peacemaker", etc.. It was a proprietary cartridge by Colt. They did not allow other firms to chamber it for some time and when they could, they did not need to due to their own developments. Both the cartridge and revolver were used by the U.S. Army from 1875 to 1892. The .45 Colt is still a popular cartridge and rifles are now chambered for it.

[7] Based on a picture of a .45 Colt cartridge sans headstamp and a similar sized copper primer in Suydam (1979: 232), this cartridge was possibly manufactured by the American Metallic Cartridge Co. The Company Incorporated in New York on April 30, 1867. It operated until circa 1870 (Barber 1987: 26). No other information is available.

[8] UMC = Union Metallic Cartridge Company. In 1854, the largest sporting goods store in the world was located in New York City; the Schuyler, Hartley and Graham Sporting Goods Co. During the Civil War, Hartley, the company's buyer, was given the temporary rank of brigadier general by the U.S. government, and became the principal purchasing agent for military arms and equipment. In 1866, the company acquired two small rimfire cartridge companies, C.D. Leet of Springfield, and the Massachusetts & Crittenden and Tibbals Manufacturing Co. of South Coventry, Connecticut. After these acquisitions the Company became the Union Metallic Cartridge and Cap Co. of Bridgeport, Connecticut. In August of 1867, the company changed its name to the Union Metallic Cartridge Co. In 1911 the merger of UMC and Remington resulted in a new company, Remington Arms – Union Metallic Company. The two companies operated separately until incorporation in 1916.

[9] As far as the author can determine, production of center-fire cartridges by the Union Metallic Cartridge Co. began sometime after 1868.

[10] A Union Metallic Cartridge Co. illustrated catalog from 1910 shows a .45 caliber Colt cartridge with a similar headstamp. At the time, this cartridge was sold with a choice of four different loadings (variants):

1. 40 grains of black powder, 250 grain inside lubricated lead bullet, No. 2 copper primer.
2. 35 grains of black powder, same bullet and primer.
3. 28 grains of black powder, same bullet and primer.
4. Smokeless powder, same bullet, No. 7 copper primer.

Table 3.11: Lead Cartridge Bullets

Catalog #	Unit	Level	Depth	Grain Weight	Caliber	Description	Firearm Signatures	Comments
853	AH	2	5-10 cm	38.7	.22	0.223"Ø X 0.500" long (pre-impact). Heeled, dish based, round nose, outside lubricated, 2 knurled cannelures above crimp groove.	Only 1 right hand twist rifling groove visible, approximately 0.060" wide.	Initial impact was probably at ogive which is obliquely flattened. Bullet probably tumbled after initial impact and struck one or more additional objects before coming to rest, resulting in body flattening and stretching. This bullet originated in a .22 Long Rifle rimfire cartridge.
2847	MDS #9	-	-	36.1	.22	Same	6 right hand twist rifling grooves, approximately 0.060" wide each.	Ogive obliquely flattened by impact, no other damage visible. These two bullets are combined because they share common attributes. They were probably manufactured by the same company and fired in the same gun.
2496	AD	4	15-20 cm	201.1	.44(?)	Because of body flattening due to impact, original diameter is undeterminable, but approximately 0.430", with a post impact length of 0.649". Flat base, pointed nose, inside lubricated. 1 knurled cannelure below crimp groove.	What is possibly a rifling groove is visible between the base and cannelure, approximately 0.136" wide, twist direction indeterminable.	This bullet is oxidized and extensively damaged by impact. It probably tumbled after initial impact and struck one or more additional objects before coming to rest. It is possibly .44 caliber and originated in a rimfire or center-fire cartridge.

Table 3.12: Shotshell

Catalog #	Unit	Level	Depth	Gauge	Cup Height	Headstamp	Comments
1569	AK	3	10-15 cm	12	5/16"	WINCHESTER No 12 NEW RIVAL	Manufacturer: Winchester Repeating Arms Company. Brand name: "New Rival" Paper tube color: Olive green. Changed to blue in 1920. Years sold: 1897-1929 (loaded with black powder). Years primed empties[1] sold: 1897-1920. The "New Rival" trademark was registered by W.R.A. Co. on 8-1-1905.

[1] A case with primer, but lacking powder or shot and sold to sportsman who preferred to load (called handloading) their own shotshell. The case represents nearly one-half the total cost of a shotshell. Handloaded shotshells can be produced for significantly less cost than factory loaded shotshells. So long as a center-fire cartridge case is in good condition, by replacing the primer, powder and bullet, it can be used repeatedly.

Table 3.13: Gun Parts

Catalog #	Unit	Level	Depth	Item	Material	Firearm Affiliation	Comments	Figure #
333 1143	Test Trench AA	- 1	- 0-5 cm	Patchbox Lid Patchbox Lid Hinge	Brass Brass	Unknown, but possibly a Kentucky Rifle[1]	These two items are combined; at one time they were held together by a hinge pin. The tang of the lid hinge is missing and probably had a 3rd screw hole. A rusty circular spot on the underside of the lids distal end was the location of a missing release pin of approximately 0.0625"Ø.	3.13.1 3.13.1
1157	AA	2	5-10 cm	Trigger Guard	Ferrous Metal	Unknown, but possibly some type of non-military muzzle-loading firearm, such as a Fowler.	The bow on this guard is rather robust. The rear tang is broken off and probably had a screw hole. There is a hole on the front tang just forward of the bow. This is possibly a screw hole; however, the curve of the bow would restrict access to this screw with a screw driver. There appears to be a rusted over screw hole at the base of the front tang's "spear-headed" finial.	3.13.3 3.13.4
1365	T	5	20-25 cm	Trigger Guard	Brass	British "Brown Bess" India Pattern Musket[2]	Rear tang broken off at the screw hole. A fragment of the sling swivel pin remains in the sling swivel hole. On the underside just forward of the fastening lug on the front tang is a "broad arrow" emblem used by the British to signify the King's property (Darling 1970: 33, Hanson 1992: 54).	3.13.5 3.13.6

Table 3.13 (continued)

	Test Trench							
1792	-	-	-	Trigger Guard	Heavily Corroded Metal	Unknown, but possibly a Model 1816 U.S. Flintlock Musket.[3]	Rear of the bow is missing. Front tang is broken off at the screw hole. A fragment of the sling swivel pin remains in the sling swivel hole. Conserved in microcrystalline wax.	3.13.7
1924	T	5	20-25 cm	Gun Flint Pad[4]	Lead	Musket	This item is incomplete, representing only half of the original pad. It probably broke in half because of its thinness, approx. 0.060", and the necessity of bending it in the middle to wrap it around a gun flint.	3.13.8
2061	CA	6	25-30 cm	Flintlock	Heavily Corroded Metal & Brass	Possibly a Model 1816 U.S. Flintlock Musket[5].	The cock is at an unnatural angle backwards past the cocked position probably due to a break in the lock works. The flash pan is brass and unfenced and tilts upward toward the rear. Conserved in microcrystalline wax.	3.13.9 3.13.10
2637	AU	5	20-25 cm	Butt Plate	Unknown	Unknown, but probably a military muzzle-loading firearm.	The tang is broken off at the screw hole. The number "215" is stamped on the inside.	3.13.11 3.13.12

[1] Initially, it was thought that these two artifacts came from a Model 1803 U.S. Flintlock Rifle. However, the Powell Site patchbox lid/lid hinge is wider at the base than the 1803. Research has shown that this style of patchbox lid/lid hinge (with slight variations) was common to various makers of Kentucky Rifles. A U.S. Contract (circa 1792-1809) rifle made by Jacob Dickert (1740-1822) and based on the Kentucky Rifle pattern has a patchbox lid/lid hinge similar to the Powell site specimen (Flayderman 1998: 491).

[2] That this trigger guard was found on the site is probably due to the Mexican Army's occupation of the Powell property in April, 1836. Houston Archeological Society member Joe Hudgins, stated that when he did a preliminary investigation of the site prior to HAS's decision to search for the Powell house, there was a butt plate and two other Brown Bess musket parts lying on the ground under a Bois d'Arc tree (the site's initial datum before being struck by lightning). These three artifacts eventually disappeared.

[3] Although badly deteriorated, the front curve of the bow and the location of the sling swivel hole are similar to a Model 1816 U.S. Flintlock Musket. Perhaps, it came from the same gun as Catalog #2061.

[4] This is another artifact possibly indicating the Mexican Army's presence on the site. Lead gunflint pads similar to this specimen have been found at other Mexican Army sites, one from 41WH92 (Mar de Lodo) and four from 41BX677 (La Villita Earthworks).

[5] There is an interesting story that goes along with this artifact. Several years after the Powell site was excavated. the author was in the HAS lab examining a box of rusty metal items from the site that had previously been deemed unidentifiable. One item in particular was dirt incrusted and measured approximately 5" long, .3/4" wide and 1-3/4" high on one end, tapering down to 5/8" on the other. There was a little lime green discoloration on one side. After holding the artifact in his hand and studying it for awhile, the author suddenly realized, and with a start, that he was holding a flintlock with a brass flash pan. After conservation, the brass flash pan was fully exposed revealing that it was unfenced. Although this flintlock has deteriorated almost beyond recognition, the opinion that this is from a Model 1816 U.S. Flintlock Musket is based on several factors: the tilting unfenced brass flash pan, rounded rear section of the lock plate, shape of the cock and the quantity of these guns produced, 325, 000 at Springfield Armory and over 350,000 at Harper's Ferry Armory, circa 1816-1840 (Flayderman 1998: 443). It should be noted however that several U.S. martial guns had flintlocks with the same general shape with an unfenced brass flashpan as the 1816 musket: the Model 1816 Pistol, Model 1817 Artillery Musket and the Model 1819 pistol. Even a few French military firearms from the 2nd half of the 1700s had flintlocks similar to the 1816. Three Model U.S. 1816 Musket flintlocks were found at site 41WH16 (Post West Bernard 1837-1839).

Table 3.14 Powder Charge Measure

Catalog #	Unit	Level	Depth	Material	Comments	Figure #
1066	AI	3	10-15 cm	Tooth	The proximal end is broken. There is a circumferential groove carved on the distal end, for the attachment of a cord whose other end was probably tied to a powder horn or shot pouch.	3.14

HOW A SPHERICAL LEAD BULLET IS MADE

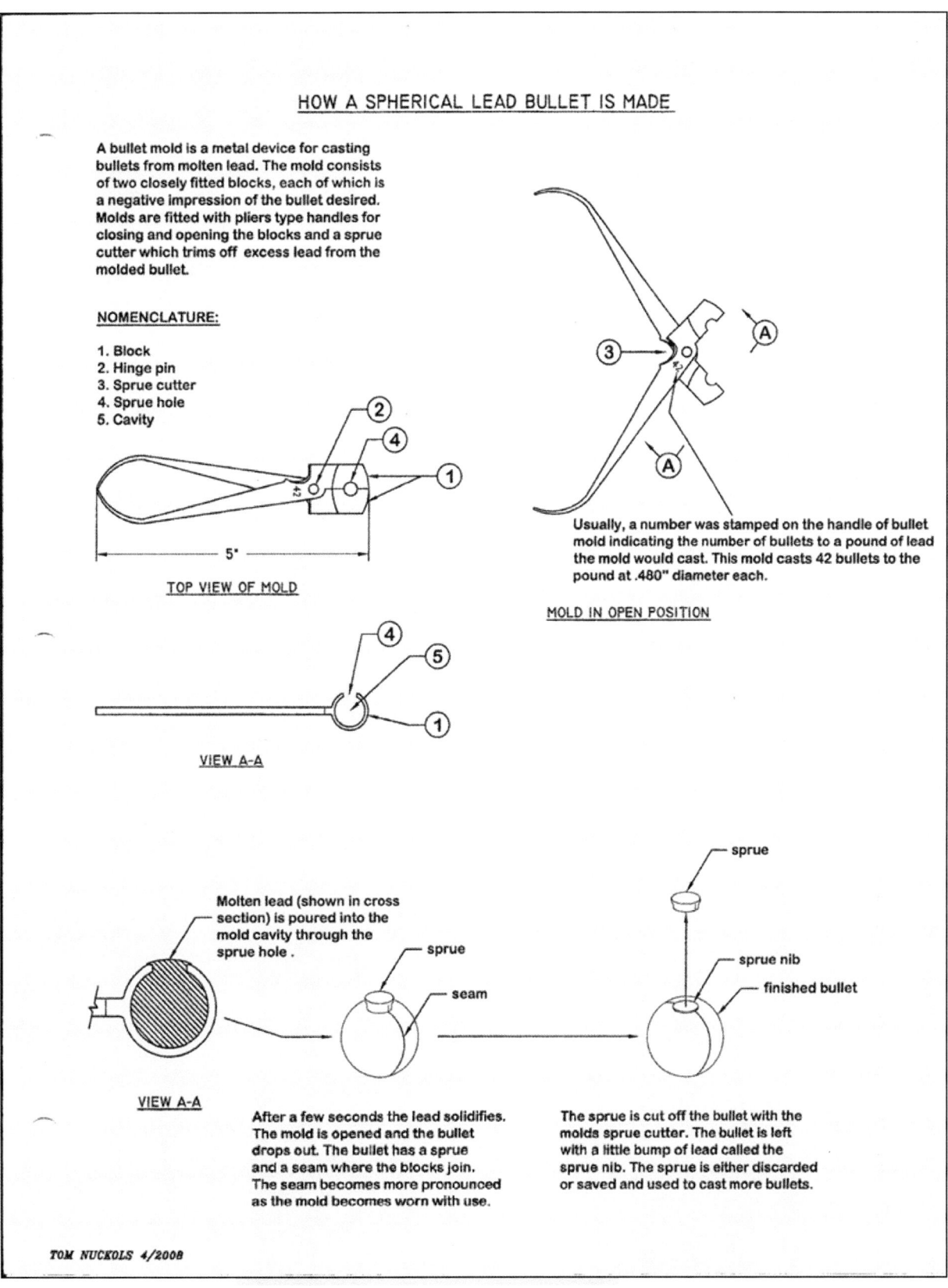

A bullet mold is a metal device for casting bullets from molten lead. The mold consists of two closely fitted blocks, each of which is a negative impression of the bullet desired. Molds are fitted with pliers type handles for closing and opening the blocks and a sprue cutter which trims off excess lead from the molded bullet.

NOMENCLATURE:

1. Block
2. Hinge pin
3. Sprue cutter
4. Sprue hole
5. Cavity

TOP VIEW OF MOLD

VIEW A-A

Usually, a number was stamped on the handle of bullet mold indicating the number of bullets to a pound of lead the mold would cast. This mold casts 42 bullets to the pound at .480" diameter each.

MOLD IN OPEN POSITION

VIEW A-A

Molten lead (shown in cross section) is poured into the mold cavity through the sprue hole.

After a few seconds the lead solidifies. The mold is opened and the bullet drops out. The bullet has a sprue and a seam where the blocks join. The seam becomes more pronounced as the mold becomes worn with use.

The sprue is cut off the bullet with the molds sprue cutter. The bullet is left with a little bump of lead called the sprue nib. The sprue is either discarded or saved and used to cast more bullets.

TOM NUCKOLS 4/2008

Illustration 3.1 How a Spherical Lead Bullet is Made

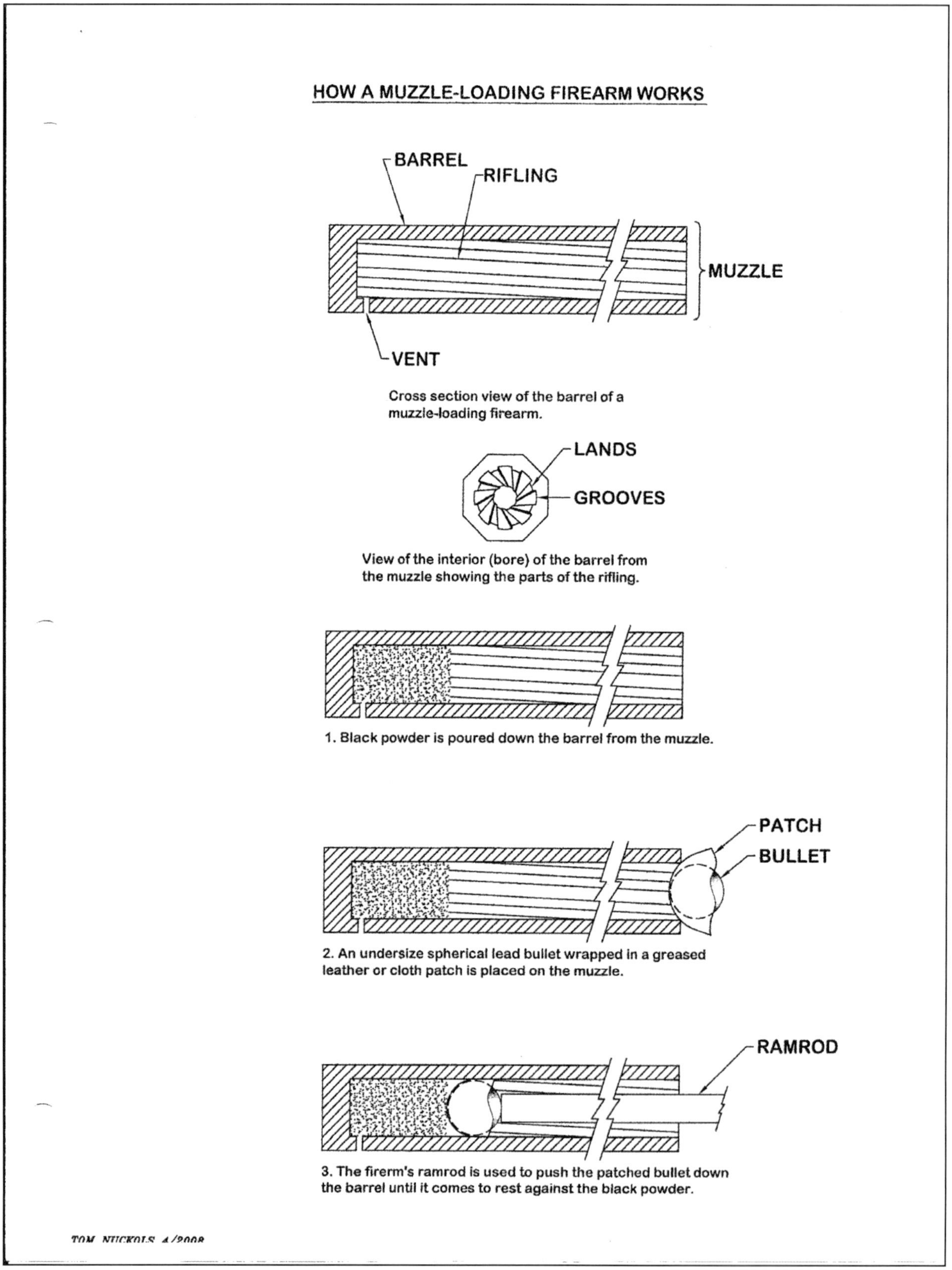

HOW A MUZZLE-LOADING FIREARM WORKS

Cross section view of the barrel of a muzzle-loading firearm.

View of the interior (bore) of the barrel from the muzzle showing the parts of the rifling.

1. Black powder is poured down the barrel from the muzzle.

2. An undersize spherical lead bullet wrapped in a greased leather or cloth patch is placed on the muzzle.

3. The firerm's ramrod is used to push the patched bullet down the barrel until it comes to rest against the black powder.

TOM NUCKOLS 4/2008

Illustration 3.2 How a Muzzle-Loading Firearm Works

HOW A MUZZLE LOADING FIREARM WORKS

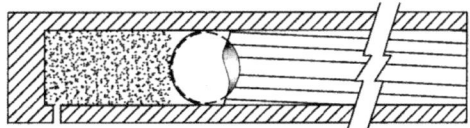

4. The ramrod is withdrawn; the gun is ready to fire.

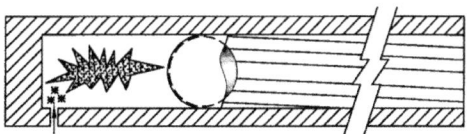

5. When the firearms trigger is pulled, it activates the ignition system which sends sparks through the vent igniting the powder.

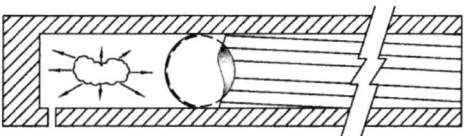

6. Ignition of the balck powder creates pressure.

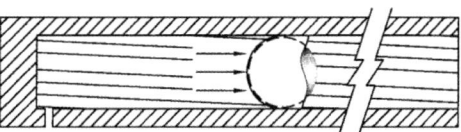

7. The pressure pushes the bullet out with force. As the bullet travels down the barrel, the rifling imparts a spin to the bullet via the patch, stabelizing its flight.

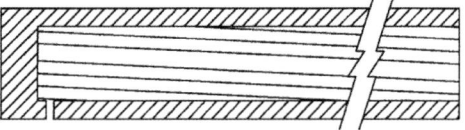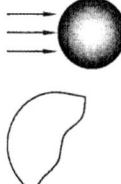

8. The speeding bullet exits the barrel. The patch falls to the ground a few feet from the muzzle.

TOM NUCKOLS 4/2008

Illustration 3.2 (continued)

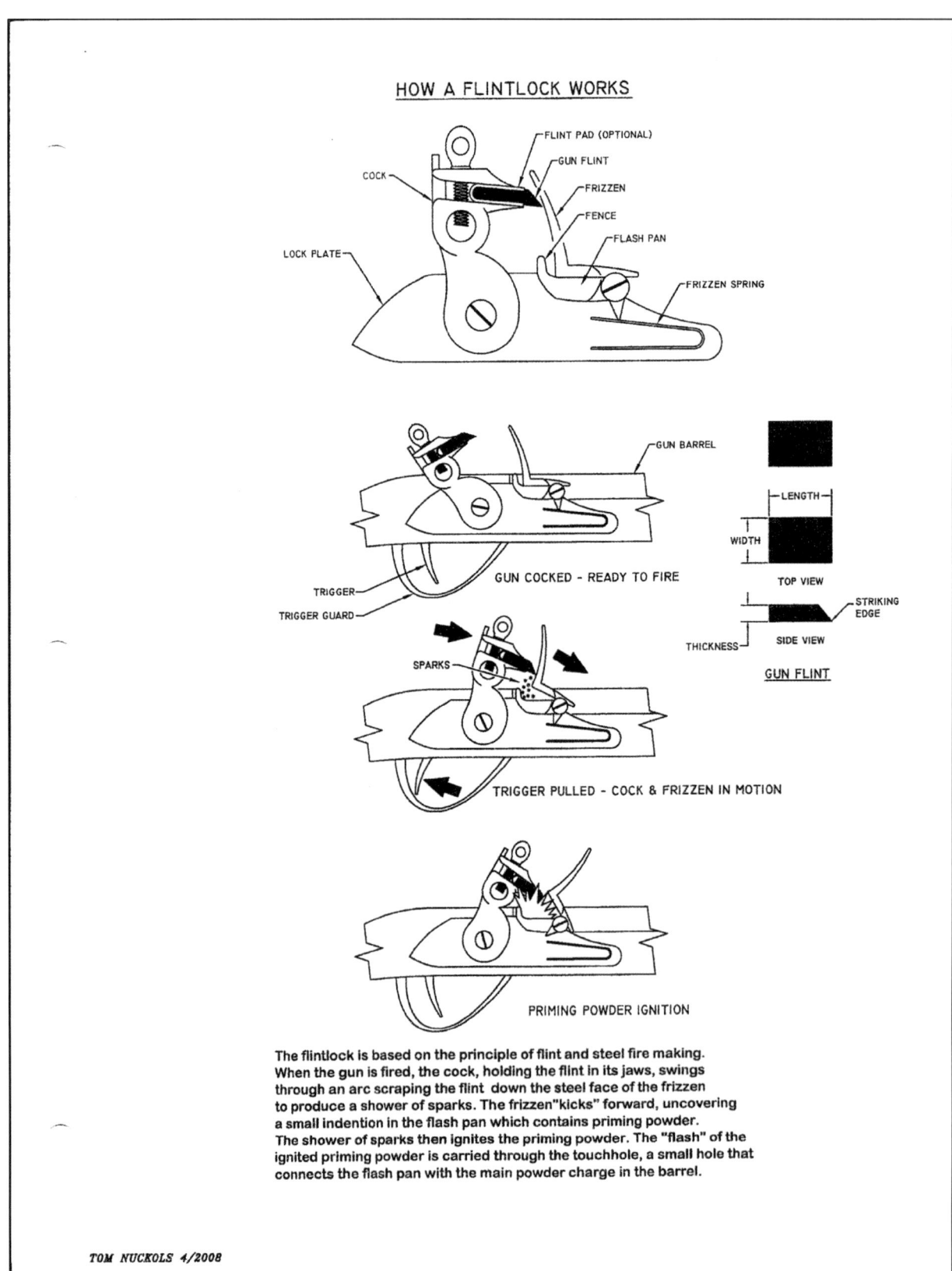

The flintlock is based on the principle of flint and steel fire making.
When the gun is fired, the cock, holding the flint in its jaws, swings
through an arc scraping the flint down the steel face of the frizzen
to produce a shower of sparks. The frizzen"kicks" forward, uncovering
a small indention in the flash pan which contains priming powder.
The shower of sparks then ignites the priming powder. The "flash" of the
ignited priming powder is carried through the touchhole, a small hole that
connects the flash pan with the main powder charge in the barrel.

TOM NUCKOLS 4/2008

Illustration 3.4 How a Flintlock Works

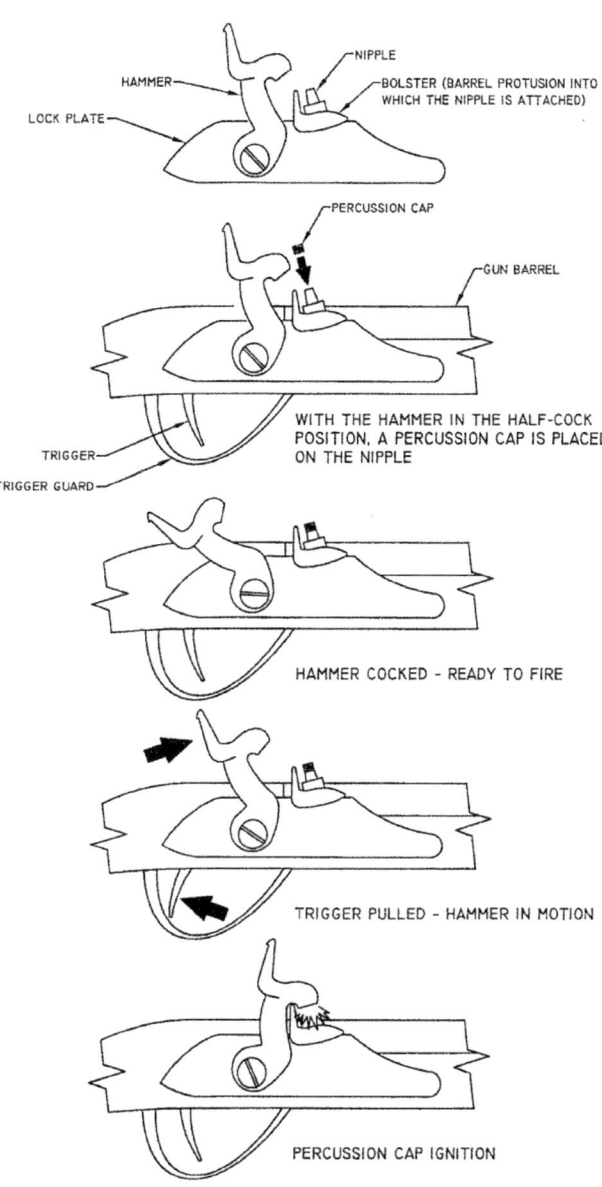

The percussion cap is placed over a hollow metal nipple at the rear of the gun barrel. Pulling the trigger releases the hammer which strikes the percussion cap, and ignites the explosive material. The flame travels through the hollow nipple to ignite the main powder charge in the barrel.

TOM NUCKOLS 4/2008

Illustration 3.7 How a Caplock (Percussion Cap) Works

CAP & BALL REVOLVER

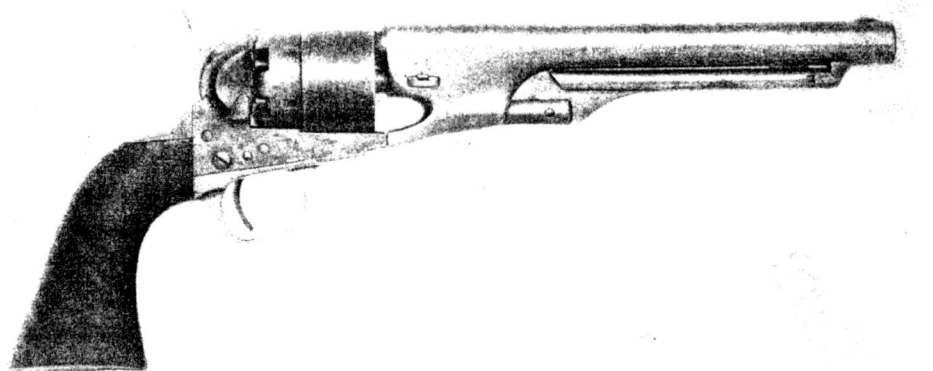

A SIX SHOT CAP & BALL REVOLVER

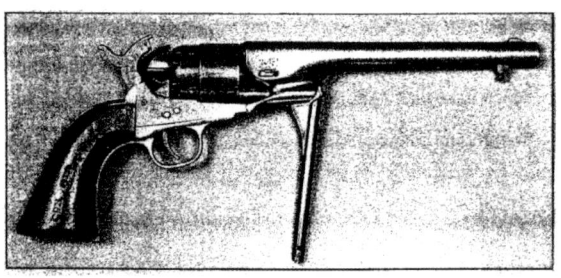

With hammer at half cock, the cylinder
rotates freely to allow loading of the lead
bullets in the front of the cylinder and
capping of the nipples on the rear of the
cyllinder. The loading lever is shown
dropped, forcing the rammer back to
seat a bullet in the chamber. This was
repeated six times to load all six chambers.

Illustration 3.8 Cap and Ball (Percussion) Revolver

HOW A CAP AND BALL REVOLVER WORKS

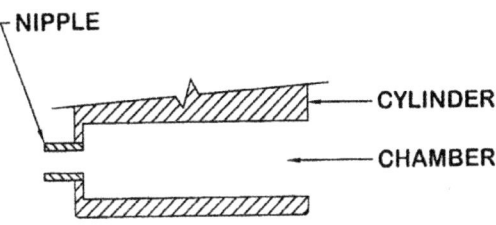

1. Cross section view of a single empty chamber in a six shot revolver.

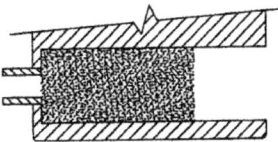

2. Black powder is poured in the front of the chamber.

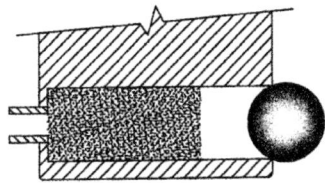

3. An oversize spherical lead bullet is placed at the mouth of the chamber.

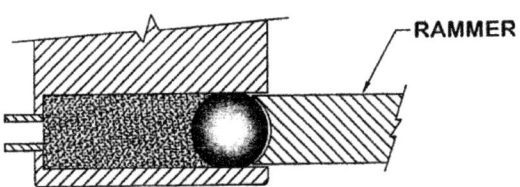

4. The rammer on the loading lever is used to force the bullet into the chamber. The bullet is deformed in the process and is left with a circular imprint from the rammer. The tight fit of the bullet is necessary to insure that it stays in place, especially when the revolver recoils when fired.

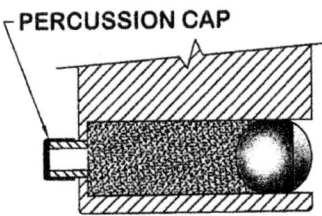

5. After the bullet is seated in the chamber, a percussion cap is placed on the nipple.

TOM NUCKOLS 4/2008

Illustration 3.8.1 How a Cap and Ball (Percussion) Revolver Works

HOW A CAP AND BALL REVOLVER WORKS

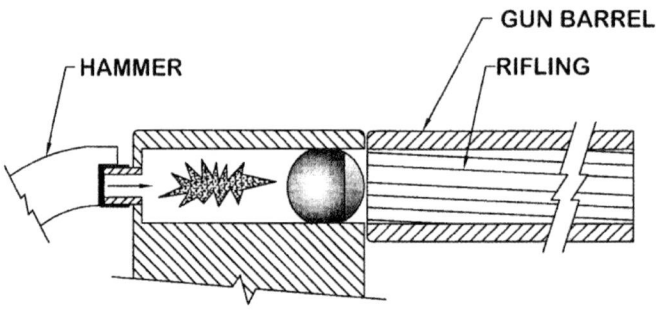

6. When the revolvers trigger is pulled, it releases the hammer. The hammer strikes the percussion cap causing it to ignite, which in turn ignites the black powder.

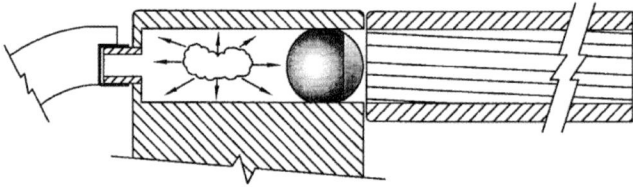

7. Ignition of the black powder creates pressure.

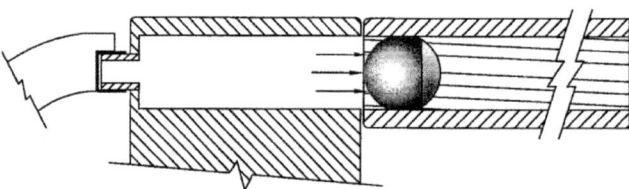

8. The pressure pushes the bullet out with force. As the bullet travels down the barrel, the rifling imparts a spin to the bullet stabelizing it's flight.

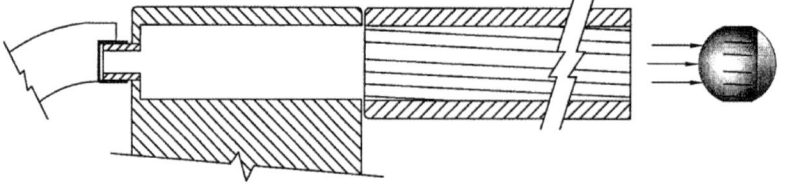

9. The speeding bullet exits the barrel and is left with an imprint of the rifling and the loading levers rammer.

TOM NUCKOLS 4/2008

Illustration 3.8.1 (continued)

Glossary

Black Powder – The oldest small arms propellant, consisting of a mechanical mixture of charcoal, sulfur and saltpeter and developed by the Chinese sometime during the 10th century (Kelly 2004). So named because of its color, black powder is considered a "low explosive" and will –unlike smokeless powder- detonate if ignited unconfined (Nonte 1973: 28).

Granulation sizes of black powder are:

Fg – For large bore shotguns, muskets and cannons.

FFg – For .50 caliber rifles or over and small gauge shotguns.

FFFg – For percussion revolvers, pistols, rifles smaller than .50 caliber, rimfire and center-fire cartridges.

FFFFg – Flintlock priming.

Passes opening of	Will not pass opening of
Fg 0.0689"	0.0582"
FFg 0.0582"	0.0376"
FFFg 0.0376"	0.0170"
FFFFg 0.0170"	0.0111"

Bore – The interior of the barrel of a gun.

Breech – The rear portion of a gun barrel.

Brown Bess – A term applied to all British flintlock muskets of the 1720-1840 period. Darling (1970: 14) states that the term "Brown Bess" became an expression of endearment, its true meaning obscured by time. Ahern (2005: 24) says that one entertaining but unlikely theory is that "Brown Bess" originated from the term "Brown Bill," which was used to describe a staff with a long blade attached. The blades on these weapons were painted brown and they were carried by British pikemen before the soldiers were issued muskets. Worman (2007: 13-14) states that the earliest use of the term "Brown Bess" was in the early 1770s, and the nickname originated from the color of the stock which in the early 1700s replaced beech wood painted black, or the rust brown staining of the barrels.

"Bess" probably was an anglicized version of the German "busche" for gun.

Butt Plate – A protective plate attached to a gun's butt to protect the wooden stock.

Cartridge – A complete unit of ammunition including bullet, metallic (brass or copper) case, powder and primer. Originally, rim and center-fire cartridges were termed "metallics" (i.e. metallic rimfire cartridge, metallic center-fire cartridge) to distinguish them from paper cartridges. Paper cartridges were a common type of ammunition used with military muzzle-loading muskets. They consisted of a bullet and powder charge wrapped in paper and required the soldier to open (usually tearing it open with the teeth) and pouring the powder down the barrel, followed by the bullet, usually still wrapped in the paper. .

Cannelure (bullet) – A circumferential groove(s) on a lead bullet to provide a reservoir for lubricant. Plain lubricating grooves on bullets began in 1857 and lasted until the end of the 1870s, being replaced by knurled grooves, which were believed to hold the lubricant more firmly (Barber 1987:169).

Cannelure (cartridge case) – A circumferential groove (plain or knurled) on a cartridge case that serves as a decoration or a seat against which the base of the bullet rests. The case cannelure is commonly found on cartridges originally designed for black powder that use smokeless powder. Due to the fewer grains of powder used with smokeless powder, a gap was left between the powder charge and bullet on black powder originated cartridges. The cannelure kept the bullet from working down into the case. The case cannelure was patented by Thomas Rylands on June 12, 1900 (Shuey 1999: 19).

Crimp – Inward bending of a case mouth into the bullet to hold it in the cartridge case.

Combustible cartridge – A case attached to a bullet and made of thin nitrated paper, linen, membrane, collodion or other substance that would be completely consumed by the powder charge explosion. It did not need to be opened to expose the powder, and was ignited by the flame from a percussion cap (Coates & Thomas 1990: 67).

Extractor – The mechanical device that removes a fired cartridge case from a firearm.

Firearm Signatures – The firing pin imprint and extractor marks on a cartridge. The rifling imprints or rammer (percussion revolver) imprint on bullets.

Firing Pin – That part of a gun which strikes the primer to fire the cartridge.

Fowler – A utilitarian civilian smoothbore (usually .75" diameter) flintlock muzzle-loader used for protection, hunting fowl (hence the name) with shot or large game using a single ball. They existed in one form or another nearly from the beginning of firearms and were the ancient counterpart of today's shotgun. Fowlers were graceful, longer and lighter than military muskets and had robust trigger guards. Fowlers probably represent the first guns to be made in what would become the United States. However, many fowlers were imported from England and France even after fabrication in the colonies began in the early 1700s (Worman 2007: 14-15).

Grain – (gunpowder) A single particle, the size of which varies according to requirements. This applies to both black and smokeless powder. For example, one of the unfired muzzle-loading bullets recovered at the Powell Site, catalog #1076-1, has an approximate diameter of .479". This bullet was probably intended for use in a rifle. A charge ranging from 60 to 80 grains of FFFg black powder would be an efficient load to fire this bullet. The .243 caliber center fire cartridge (case) recovered, catalog #2855, would have contained (depending on the gun powder brand) 35 to 44 grains of smokeless gun powder.

Grain – (lead) a unit of weight, 0.0022857 ounce, in avoirdupois. Bullet weights and lead objects are expressed in grains. As a point of reference, there are 437.5 grains per ounce. Although the weight may vary, depending on manufacturer, a modern .38 Special revolver bullet weighs approximatley130 grains.

Gun Flint Pad – A lead pad for holding a gun flint securely in the jaws of a flintlock cock.

Headstamp – The marking impressed upon the base of the cartridge by the maker. It can indicate who made the cartridge, the caliber, when it was made, the brand, a decoration, or as much information as space allows and the maker decides to put there (Hogg 1982: 35).

Inside lubricated – Description for a cylindro-conical lead bullet whose cannelure(s) are located below the cartridge case mouth.

Kentucky Rifle – Circa 1720-1850. An American development of the muzzle-loading flintlock period generally conceded to have evolved from the short heavy Jaeger rifles brought to North America by German colonists. The term "Kentucky" developed because of the area in which the rifle was widely used, not because it was manufactured there. Development was seated principally in Pennsylvania. The Kentucky rifle used a long barrel of medium bore and was stocked to the muzzle. Stocks were slender and of delicate construction with a deep crescent butt plate and a patch box, usually with a brass lid, on the right side (Nonte 1973: 144).

Kentucky Pistol – A muzzle-loading, single shot pistol contemporary with the Kentucky rifle and sharing its style and characteristics.

Misfire – The failure of a cartridge to fire. A rimfire cartridge can be re-chambered (rotated in the chamber so that the firing pin strikes the primer in a different location) in an attempt to get the cartridge to fire. This endeavor is usually successful.

Musket – A smoothbore shoulder arm that fires a spherical lead ball.

Muzzle – The front of a gun barrel.

Muzzle-loader – Any gun with a solid breech which must be loaded through the muzzle by first pouring in a charge of black powder, followed by a bullet.

Ogive – The curved, rounded, or pointed forward portion of a bullet.

Patchbox – A rectangular cavity in the butt stock of both civilian and military muzzle-loading firearms. As the name implies, patchboxes were originally devised to hold greased cloth patches with which to insert the bullet more easily in the rifled bore and hold it tight. Patchboxes were, however, multi-purpose and held many other small articles and accessories: spare flints, percussion caps, small tools, etc. (Flayderman1998: 539). Patchboxes were covered with a hinged lid, usually made of sheet brass.

Pistol – A single-shot firearm with either a smooth or rifled bore. The term pistol and revolver are often used synonymously.

Powder Flask - A container for carrying black powder to be used in muzzle-loading firearms and made of copper or other non-sparking metal. Powder flasks had a spout that metered predetermined charges of black powder by volume.

Powder Horn - A container for carrying black powder used in muzzle-loading firearms and usually made from a cow's horn that had been scraped thin, plugged at one end and with a stopper at the other. The average length of a powder horn was 11" and their capacity was from one-half to three-quarters of a pound of black powder. Powder horns were equipped with a leather strap for carrying over the shoulder. The powder horn was in general use until the end of the flintlock era. It was superseded by the powder flask which came in with the percussion period and passed with it (Dillin 1967: 149-151).

Revolver – A handgun in which the bullets or cartridges are contained in separate chambers (usually 6) of a cylinder behind the barrel. With a few exceptions, revolvers have rifled bores. The term revolver and pistol are often used synonymously.

Ribbed – Circumferential ridges on a percussion cap.

Rifle – A shoulder arm with a rifled bore.

Shot Bag – An essential accoutrement of the era of the Kentucky rifle. Because of the style of clothing of the period that men wore, they needed some means to carry their supplies and personal items. The shot pouch became their pocket and in them were carried bullets, bullet patches, gun flints, gun cleaning materials, small tools, etc. Shot bags were often made of dressed buckskin and had a leather strap for carrying over the shoulder. Shot bags were also called bullet pouches, hunting pouches, shooting bags or sporting bags.

Smokeless powder – The modern propellant for all small arms ammunition, invented in the mid 1880s and first used widely in this country in the early 1890s. The first cartridges to use smokeless powder in the U.S. were the .30-40 service rifle cartridge in 1892 and the .30-30 Winchester in 1895.

Variant – Loading variations in the individual components that make up a particular caliber of center-fire cartridge such as bullet style or weight, powder charge or powder type (black or smokeless), etc. Variants are identified by the manufacturer in several ways, especially via the headstamp, the size of letters or numbers, punctuation, periods or placement of periods or hyphens. Primer size was also a good variant indicator.

Chapter 4
Miscellaneous Faunal, Slate, and Shell Artifacts

By Elizabeth K. Aucoin
Photography by Linda L. Swift

Introduction

This chapter will focus on three types of miscellaneous artifacts, namely faunal material, slate and slate pencils, and shells recovered during excavations at the Elizabeth Powell site.

Faunal Material

Four thousand six hundred and thirty pieces of faunal material (Table 4.1) were recovered from across the Powell site. While many of the fragments were too small to be identified, Houston Archeological Society member Joe Hudgins' initial analysis identified sub-adult pig bones, a tooth, and two tusks, as well as bird bones and a catfish vertebra. Catfish are still present in the waters of Turkey Creek. Additional analysis by the author revealed the presence of deer, bird, turtle, two unidentified fish scales, and possibly a cow bone with visible cut marks.

Four hundred and twenty fragments, or 9.1% of the total 4630, were recovered from excavations near Turkey Creek (West section), while 4210 fragments or 90.9% of the total were recovered from the upland or East section of the site. Located within the West section is Trash Pit #2 comprised of eight pits: AA, AI, AM, BD, BE, DA, EA, and EB. Three hundred and eighty-five pieces of faunal material (91.7% of 420) were recovered from this trash pit. The remaining 35 pieces (8.3%) were recovered from the ninth pit (EC).

In the East section of the site is located Trash Pit #1 comprised of five pits: E, S, T, AK, and BH. Twelve hundred and forty-five faunal pieces (29.6% of 4210) were found in this trash pit with the greatest concentration in pit T (N=436). An additional 561 pieces (13.3% of 4210) were recovered from six 50x100cm pits (M1-M6) excavated in May 1999; unfortunately, those pits were not recorded on the site map and their exact location is currently unknown.

The greatest concentration of faunal material across the entire site was found in Level 4 (1121 pieces or 24.2%) at a depth of 15-20 cm followed by Level 3 containing 996 pieces or 21.5% at a depth of 10-15cm.

Slate and Slate Pencils

Webster's New Twentieth Century Dictionary defines slate as "a kind of hard, fine-grained rock that cleaves (splits) naturally into thin, smooth-surfaced layers" (1983:1705). The color of slate varies from dark gray to bluish gray, to dark bluish

Figure 4.1 Slate Fragments

or dark purplish gray. Pieces of this material can be used as a writing surface, while softer pieces of slate were fashioned into thin, cylindrical pointed writing implements (pencils) for use on writing slates.

The Early Office Museum website indicates that "during the second half of the 19th and early 20th century, pencils cut from solid pieces of softer grades of slate or soap-stone were used by school children to write on tables cut from harder grades of slate."

A total of 82 fragments of slate and slate pencils were recovered during excavations at the site. All of the slate artifacts, comprised of 75

Figure 4.2 Homemade Pencil

pieces of slate and 7 slate pencil fragments (Figure 2), were recovered from the East section of the site and were dark gray in color. Six of the seven pencils were cylindrical in shape while the seventh pencil appears to have been fashioned from a flat piece of slate. One end of the seventh pencil is rounded and smoothed from use, as are the sides where someone's fingers might have gripped the pencil while practicing a writing task or recording some type of information.

The slate fragments were sized using a hand-drawn template of squares ranging in size from <15 millimeters square to 25-30 millimeters square. Most of the fragments were in the <15 millimeters square range and none measured larger than 20-25 millimeters square. Thickness of the flat fragments ranged from 1-4 millimeters. The pencil fragments ranged from 12-29 millimeters in length and 3-5 millimeters in diameter. The seventh or "home-made" pencil measured 14 millimeters long, 7 millimeters wide, and 2 millimeters thick.

Twenty-four of the fragments were recovered from Trash Pit #1 comprised of five units: E, S, T, AK, and BH. Eleven fragments came from pits BA, BB, and BC, while seven were found while excavating the Cistern. Fragments from these areas, N-48, represent 59% of the total slate found across the eastern section of the site.

Shells

During a visit to the Brazosport Museum of Natural Science in Clute, Texas, the author was very fortunate to meet Betty Bickman, Assistant Curator of Malacology, who was arranging an exhibit of Hawaiian shells. Ms. Bickman graciously agreed to identify the shells in the author's possession that had not previously been identified through the use of books and the author's own shell collection from Galveston area beaches.

A total of 22 sea shells (2 complete and 20 fragments) were recovered from the site (Table 4.2). One complete disk dosinia half shell and 3 shell fragments of a disk dosinia were found in Pit EC, levels 4 and 5, in the West section of the site located near Turkey Creek. The remaining shells were from the East or upland section of the site. Disk dosinia is a bivalve as are clams, cockles, and oysters.

Of the 18 shells and shell fragments from the upland area, the specimens recovered were gastropods (univalve or one shell) and bivalves. The gastropod fragments were identified as lightning whelk, the Texas State Shell, and scotch bonnet, while the bivalve specimens included quahog, blood ark, disk dosinia, and yellow cockle. Four of the fragments, including two burned cockle shells, were too small to further identify. The fragments too small to identify are probably marine (sea) shells rather than riverine shells since no identifiable riverine shells were recovered. There was no concentration of shells in any given pit but were found scattered across the site.

References and Other Resources

Andrews, Jean
    1975   *Sea Shells of the Texas Coast.* University of Texas Press, Austin, TX and London, England
    1992   *A Field Guide to Shells of the Texas Coast.* Gulf Publishing Company, Houston, TX

Bickham, Betty
    2008   Personal interview on April 5, 2008 at the Brazosport Museum of Natural Science, Clute, TX

Early Office Museum Contributors "Slate Pencils"
    n.d.   Slate Pencils, http://www.officemuseum.com/pencil_history.htm. Accessed 4/3/2008

SHG Resources Contributors "Texas Symbols, Shell: Lightning Whelk"
    2008   Lightning Whelk, http://shgrresources.com/tx/symbols/shell. Accessed 4/5/2008

Texas Parks and Wildlife Contributors "Lightning Whelk (*Busycon perversum pulleyi*)"
    2007   Lightning Whelk, http://tpwd.state.tx.us/huntwild/species/lwhelk. Accessed 4/5/2008

Webster's New Twentieth Century Dictionary, Second Edition
    1983   Simon and Schuster, New York, NY

Table 4.1 Faunal Material Recovered

Pit	1	2	3	4	5	6	7	8	9	10	11	12	13	14	15	16	17	18	29	20	Total
A	1	4	11	12																	28
B	5		8																		13
C	2	7	19	32																	60
D	4	26	34	14																	78
E	11	2	11		19	13				1											57
F	6	9	13	12																	40
G	2			7																	9
H			23	5																	28
J			1	7	2																10
K	3		15				1														19
L		3	3																		6
M		3	2	10																	15
O			3	5	5	1															14
P	2	2	4	1																	9
Q		1	5																		6
S		20	7		48	5	17		13		3										113
T	12	23	17	13		148	20	26	37	25	25	36	28	26							436
U	22	39	18																		79
V			5	5	8																18
X		1		1	1																3
Y	2	1	13	7	4																27
Z			25	1	3																29
AA	7	29	66	69																	171
AB		6																			6
AC			13	1																	14
AD			2																		2
AE	12	5	18	18																	53
AF	1			8																	9
AG	3	16	24	11																	54
AH		4	22	33	18																77

Table 4.1 (continued)

AI	2	1	76	25											104
AJ		9	4			2									15
AK	24	18	30	16	46	21	21	29	19	9	17	23	17	3	293
AL	1	11	18	217											247
AM			16	3											19
AN	27	20	19												66
AO	5	30	14	30	11										90
AP	13	10	15	38	5										81
AQ		15	37	51											103
AR		13	11	19											43
AS	6	11	21	31	11										80
AT	3	2													5
AO	42	12	22	22	3										101
AX		2		14	35										51
AY	4		2	8		9									23
AZ		19	17	11	4										51
BA	10	44	5												59
BB	3	21	26												50
BC	14	36	9												59
BD	9	6	56												71
BE	1	1													2
BF		2	3	5											10
BG		5	11	15											31
BH	20	26	12	51	65	15	47		27	28	21	9	20	5	346
BJ	1	7													8
CA	7	27	68	46	58	72	37	18							333
CB		21		62											83
DA	27	7													34
EB	2	2													4
EC				8	7	20									35

Table 4.1 (continued)

																					Total
Cistern	3											2				3	2		1	16	31
Feat. 2	7																				10
South 2		5	28																		33
M1	48	37	13	25	9	13	5														150
M2	6	19	58	47	36	6															172
M3	2	15	11	12	10	3															53
M4	12	9	30	7	2																60
M5	8	14	8	44	7	8		9													98
M6	4	1	8	13								2									28
Ped Survey	11																				11
T																					
Trench	4																				4
Total	**414**	**676**	**996**	**1121**	**432**	**337**	**148**	**82**	**96**	**63**	**66**	**72**	**67**	**38**	**0**	**3**	**2**	**0**	**1**	**16**	**4630**

Table 4.2 Shells Recovered

Catalog #	Pit	Level	Common Name	Latin Name	Comments
141-1	B	2	Texas Quahog	*Mercenaria campechienis texana*	Bivalve; fragment
.141-2	B	2	unknown		too small to identify
412-1	AC	3	Texas Quahog	*Mercenaria campechienis texana*	Bivalve; complete half-shell
412-2	AC	3	Cockle		burned; too small to identify
412-3	AC	3	Cockle		burned; too small to identify
908	BH	5	Disk dosinia	*Dosinia (Dosinidia) discus*	Bivalve
930	BH	9	unknown		too small to identify
1143	BB	2	unknown		mother-of-pearl (2)
					too small to identify
1305	S	8	unknown		too small to identify (2)
1334-1	T	2	unknown		too small to identify
1334-2	T	2	unknown		mother-of-pearl
1346	T	3	Blood Ark	*Andara (Lunara) ovalis*	Bivalve
1492	T	12	Scotch Bonnet	*Phalium (Semicassis) granulatum*	Univalve; fragment
1762	BF	3	Scotch Bonnet	*Phalium (Semicassis) granulatum*	Univalve; lip only
1785	BG	4	Lightning Whelk	*Busycon perversum pulleyi*	Univalve; fragment
2062	CA	4	Cockle	*Trachycardium (Dallocardia) muricatum*	Bivalve; Yellow fragment
2063	Z	5	unknown		too small to identify
2699-1	EC	4	Disk dosinia	*Dosinia (Dosinidia) discus*	Bivalve; fragment
2699-2	EC	4	Disk dosinia	*Dosinia (Dosinidia) discus*	Bivalve; complete half-shell
2764	EC	5	Disk dosinia	*Dosinia (Dosinidia) discus*	Bivalve; fragments (2)

Chapter 5
Summary and Conclusion
By Elizabeth K. Aucoin

Elizabeth Powell, a widow with four children, entered Texas from Louisiana in November 1828 as a colonist of Stephen F. Austin. Sometime prior to March 3, 1831, she cleared a field and built her house near the banks of Turkey Creek. On March 21, 1831, her application for a land grant, signed and dated March 3, 1831, in the presence of Austin's secretary, Samuel May Williams, was approved, and she received one league of land from the Mexican government. This was the first grant in Austin's second colony in current Fort Bend County.

Madame Powell's place, as it later became known, was a convenient resting point about midway between San Felipe in present day Austin County and Columbia in present day Brazoria County. Her house was also near the junctions of routes to San Antonio, Matagorda and the trail leading to Old Fort (currently Richmond) and Harrisburg within the city limits of present day Houston. Travelers could stop at her place for a good meal and spend the night before continuing their journey the following day.

General Antonio Lopez de Santa Anna and his Mexican army also found the Powell property a convenient place to rest after traveling south from San Felipe, the settlement that had been abandoned by its residents and then burned. General Sam Houston and most of his men proceeded north from San Felipe along the west side of the Brazos River, while others crossed to the east side of the Brazos and remained behind to harass the Mexican troops while protecting the fleeing colonists. This event became known in Texas history as the "Runaway Scrape." After the battle of San Jacinto and the subsequent capture of Santa Anna on the following day, April 22, 1836, a council of war was convened at Mrs. Powell's place on April 25th. The Mexican generals decided not to pursue the war, and the Mexican Army began its orderly withdrawal to Bexar (San Antonio) and Guadalupe Victoria (in Mexico). As the troops were withdrawing on April 26th, the Powell house and other structures were burned. In 1936, as part of the Texas Centennial Celebration, the State of Texas erected an historic marker on the grounds of the Elizabeth Powell homestead. A portion of the marker's inscription reads "...This point marks the most eastern advance of (General) Urrea's army and the most southern advance of Santa Anna, who turned east from here to the Brazos and San Jacinto."

While the State of Texas marker places Elizabeth Powell's homestead in a historical context, prior to the archeological investigations undertaken by members of the Houston Archeological Society and its members' accompanying research, little was known about Elizabeth Powell and her homestead or the cultural remains deposited upon and beneath the prairie grasses. Biographical information and a historical summary on Mrs. Powell and her homestead can be found in Part 1 of the Elizabeth Powell site report published by the Houston Archeological Society in April, 2007. Part 2 of the report was published in December, 2007. This part, Part 3, is the final report to be published documenting the research and investigations undertaken at the Elizabeth Powell site.

Artifacts Recovered

A total of 30,245 artifacts were recovered from the site, and approximately 50% were analyzed. Some of the artifacts identified but not analyzed include animal bones, charcoal, bottle and window glass, pressed glass, bricks and mortar, wood, and other miscellaneous items. Analysis of the following artifacts was documented in Part 2 of the Elizabeth Powell site report or in this report, Part 3, and the possibility of attribution to the Powell occupation is indicated in each section:

- **Beads:** Four beads were found, but one diamond-faceted dark brown-black bead, whose optimal period of use was between 1805 and 1860--with a mean date of 1830, corresponds with the Powell period of occupation. (Part 2)

- **Buttons:** Fifty-eight buttons, 40 complete and 18 partial, were examined. The following buttons fit nicely with the 1828-1836 timeframe when Elizabeth Powell occupied the site: one four-hole bone button with a prick mark and six five-hole bone buttons (1750-1830); one metal fabric-covered button (1813-1825), some Golden Age gilt buttons, especially the metal Mexican Army button with the number 6 on the front (circa 1823-1832) and a probable Mexican Army button with an eagle on its front side, and some of the marine shell buttons. (Part 2)

- **Ceramics:** About 2200 sherds were recovered and distributed across the site. Many of the sherds analyzed post-date the Powell occupation; however, some of the sherds recovered tend to correspond to the pre-1836 presence of Mrs. Powell. Some of the nine deep blue styles and patterns of transferware that most likely belonged to Elizabeth Powell include Rabbit Hunting, Hunting Series by Davenport; and Game Birds pattern by Stubbs. Those patterns were recovered from what was probably a Powell occupation trash pit. Recovered from the same trash pit were two of the lighter blue patterns, Persian by Heath and the Europa pattern by Riley. (Part 3)

- **Coins:** While five coins were found, only one coin, a ½ Real bearing the Mexico City mint mark and dated 1808, can possibly be attributed to the time of the Powell occupation, as Spanish Colonial and Mexican coins were considered the "coin of the realm" at the time of the Powell occupation. These types of coins were in common use and considered legal tender until 1857 and remained in publicly accepted circulation even after 1857. The coin may have belonged to Mrs. Powell, it may have been dropped by one of the Mexican soldiers while they were at the Powell site in April 1836, or it could have belonged to someone who later occupied the property. (Part 2)

- **Metal and Miscellaneous Objects:** Two pairs of scissors and a partial candleholder were excavated and are similar to those found at an 1836 Mexican Army campsite in Wharton County. The scissors and candleholder were excavated from level 3 of two adjacent pits in the West section and located a short distance from the creek. It has been hypotesized that the candleholder from the Mexican campsite may have come from Mrs. Powell's place. (Part 3)

- **Miscellaneous Faunal, Slate and Shell:** Various types of animal bones were recovered from across the site, some with cut marks and others with evidence of burning. Slate and slate pencils were found in pits located on the eastern section of the site and probably attributable to the occupation post-dating that of Mrs. Powell. Marine shells were also found, as were some buttons made from these types of shells; however, there is no evidence to suggest that Mrs. Powell utilized those shells for making buttons. In two instances, marine shells and slate pencils or fragments were recovered from the same pits: Pit AC, Level 3, contained a slate pencil and a Quahog marine shell; Pit BG, Level 4, had fragments of a slate pencil and a Lightning Whelk shell. Both pits were located in the East section of the site. (Part 3)

- **Munitions:** Spherical muzzle-loading lead bullets, an unidentified muzzle-loading lead bullet, lead sprues, gun flints, gun parts and a powder charge measure were among the items recovered. Four mold-cast buckshot that were found most likely date to the Powell occupation. All these artifacts came from or were used in muzzle-loading firearms, and all of the gun parts are from muzzle-loading firearms and probably date to the time of the Powell occupation. (Part 3)

- **Nails:** The Powell house was probably a dogtrot log house whose construction didn't require the use of nails. Consequently, the nails found at the site were not from the Powell house but from a house later built on the property. (Part 2)

- **Prehistoric Artifacts:** A total of 192 prehistoric artifacts were recovered from across the site. While no projectile points were recovered, the assemblage included a utilized unifacial flake, a heavily-patinated biface (possibly a preform for a small dart point), a re-touched notched tool (possibly a spoke shaver) and a possible scraping tool. Nine small Goose Creek pottery sherds and fired clay balls confirm the presence of Native

Americans who probably occupied or visited this inland Southeast Texas site sometime after AD 500. (Part 2)

Extensive research and archeological excavations support historic documents that this site was the property of Elizabeth Powell and that the Mexican Army visited the site on at least two occasions. While some tantalizing clues may lead to future searches, the actual location of Mrs. Powell's home remains a mystery.

The artifacts from the Powell site remain in the possession of the Houston Archeological Society and are curated in the archaeology lab at Rice University pending final disposition of the artifacts.

Made in the USA
Charleston, SC
22 November 2014